HIS NITIMUR ET MUNITUR.

J. A. Maconochie.

Templaria.

PAPERS

RELATIVE TO THE

HISTORY, PRIVILEGES, AND POSSESSIONS

OF THE

SCOTISH KNIGHTS TEMPLAR,

AND THEIR SUCCESSORS THE

KNIGHTS OF SAINT JOHN

OF

JERUSALEM.

MDCCCXXVIII.

INFORMATION

For Ross *of* Auchlossin,

Against

The Possessors of the Temple-lands.

AUCHLOSSIN having insisted in a Reduction and Improbation against the Possessors of certain Temple-lands contained in his and his Authors Chartors and Infeftments; There was a Certification pronounced, but thereafter a Petition was given in to the Lords by certain of the Defenders, conform to a List and Condescendance, for whom It was alledged that they are not bound to take a day at the instance of this Pursuer, or satisfy the Production, because the Temple-lands fell under the Act of Annexation 1587, Whereby all Lands were annexed to the Crown, which Act was ratified and extended by the 14th Act *Parl.* 1633 ; As also by the 58 *Act Parl.* 1661 : and this Petition being once refused, but again renewed, there followed a Debate in presence upon these two points,

1. Whether Temple lands were Kirk lands, and consequently fell under the Acts of Annexation.

2. *Esto* Temple-lands were Kirk lands if they be not excepted in the Act 1587, and if that general exception be taken away by the Acts 1633 and 1661.

It

It was alledged for the Defenders, that the Order of the Templars was an Ecclesiastick Order, and their Lands and Benefices were also Ecclesiastick, first begun in the year 1118, under *Baldwin* second King of *Jerusalem*, who gave them a Habitation near the Temple, whence they afterwards took their Name of Templars, the end of the Institution was to gaird the Rodes and defend the Pilgrims that went to *Jerusalem*, and the 9 Knights first institute did take a Vow between the hands of *Garemund* the Patriarch of *Jerusalem* to live according to the Vow of the Cannons regular.

In the year 1128, they were confirmed by the Council of *Troyes* in *France*, who gave them a particular Rule and ordered a Habit, which was a white Mantle, *&c.* to which *Eugen* the *3d* not many years after added a Reid Cross, which he allowed the Knights and Priests of the Order to wear.

This military Order in a short time grew very populous and Rich, but having fallen under the Displeasure of *Philip* the fair King of *France*, & being generaly envyed for their great Possessions, they were supprest in the 14 Centurie, for the *French* King having bafled the papal Authority in the person of *Boniface* the 8. *Clement* the 5 who succeded next to him but one, and was a Creature of *France*, resolved to retrive the Papal Authority, and at the same time to gratify his Patron, which was effectual by the ruine of the Templars, wherein the Pope had also many other Advantages.

The Series of that History does sufficiently demonstrat, that as the original of the Order was Ecclesiastick ; So they enjoyed the privilege of Churchmen being exempted from Civil Jurisdiction, and therefore albeit the undoing of that Order was agreed betwixt the Pope and the King of *France*, yet the King having proceeded to seize the whole Templars in his Kingdom in one day, *viz.* the 5 of *October* 1307, or as some will have it in the 1306 ; the Pope complains by a Bull of the 27 of the same Moneth, that he had imprisoned the Templars Subjects of the Church *absque medio*, and had seized their Estates, which *did* not belong to secular power ; Therefore he sent two Cardinals to treat of the Affair, and to receive the Prisoners and their effects.

But the King of *France* having proceeded furder to enquire into the matter, the Pope inhibited the Clergy to be concerned in it,
whereupon

whereupon the King applyed to the *Sorbon*, who by their resolve 24 *March* 1308, declared *that these who are listed for the defence of the faith, and have made profession of a Religion established by the Church, ought to pass among the Religious, and enjoy the benefite of exemption, and that there Estates ought to be reserved to the ends for which they were conferred on them.*

After this resolve the King of *France* put some of the principal Templars in the hands of the Legats sent by the Pope, and the Pope being thus satisfied by a Bull the 5 of *July* 1308 allowed the Process to proceed against the Templars to sentence, reserving to himself nevertheless the Process against the great Master of the Temple, and against the Masters and Heads of the Order in *France* and beyond seas, and by four other Bulls in the same Moneth appointed their Lands to be applyed for the Relief of the Holy land, saving nevertheless the Rights which the King and other Lords might have to them.

All things being thus prepared, then in the close of the Moneth of *August* 1308, the Pope by several Bulls appointed the Archbishops and Bishops in *Christendom* to make Inquisition concerning the Templars, and to transmit their Informations, and at last in the Council of *Vienn* begun the 16 of *October* 1311 The Order was supprest by a Bull 22 *May* 1312, wherein the Pope with Approbation of the Council, not in form of a definitive Sentence, because it could not in Rigor or Justice be carried so far according to the Informations and Proceses which had been made *sed per viam provisionis Appostolicæ irrefragibili & perpetuo valetura sustulimus sanctione,* and that all their Estates should remain in the disposal of the Holy see, which Goods moveable and immoveable, by advice of the Council was unit to the Order of St. *John* of *Jerusalem* or *Hospitulars,* reserving the Goods belonging to the Templars in the Kingdoms of *Castile, Arragon, Portugal* and *Majorca* to his own Disposal, with many others.

So that from the whole account, it is evident that the Order of Templars was, as to their Institution, Ecclesiastick, and that their Goods were disposed off by the Church; As also by the Rule framed for them in the Council of *Troyes,* they were subject to the *tria vota substantialia religionis,* Poverty, Chastety, and Obedience, which are the essential Characters of Religious Orders in the

the Church of *Rome*; Likeas in the account of the History of the persecution of these Templars, mention is made of the Priests of that Order, and they have been ranked amongst Ecclesiasticks by Cannonists and Divines, and even by some Canons are reckoned so.

To all this it was answered, that the Order of the Templars being neither institute for Devotion, nor Charity, but originally for guarding of the High-roads with force of Arms, as they were called Ecclesiasticks improperly, so they were constantly called a Military Order in a true and genuine Sense; And *Tholousanus* speaking of one of the strictest of the Vowes taken by one of them, says, *Ob votum castitatis affines sunt & ecclesiasticis personis, verumtamen ecclesiasticæ personæ non sunt cum arma libere & ex professione pertractent pro fidei tuitione adversus Agarenus exemplum Machabæorum que tamen clericis non conceduntur Syntag. lib. 15. cap. 33. Numb. 3.* Nor were their Vowes proper, and strict Tyes as the Vowes of the several religious Orders for the Vow of Chastitie imported no more but continence in Marriage, and their Obedience was only Submission to the Master of their Order, as their Poverty was a Restriction not to acquire without a Dispensation from their Grand-master, which kinds of Dispensations were as often granted as required, as is observed by *Carleval de judiciis Tit.* 1. *Disput.* 2. *Sect.* 3. *Numb.* 416. In which Section the question if the Knights of these military Orders was religious, is expresly treated, and the different opinion of the *Cannonists* related ; But this in general as to their Opinion is to be observed, that as the Countreys or Orders to which they belonged are more servily subject to the Church of *Rome*, they are more inclinable to the opinion that the military Order of Knighthood are ecclesiastick, or as they are more free they incline to the Opinion that they are secular.

But this is obvious to common reason, that seing the end and essential Character of every pretended religious Order according to the opinion of Cannonists, is some singular spiritual Perfection, the military Orders whereof the end is Blood and Violence, and supposes a necessity of Resistance and Force, can never in proper Sense be called Ecclesiastick or Religious, and albeit they were tyed strictly to the Vowes, yet that not being the main end of their Institution,

stitution, but *accedens preter naturam,* they can never be properly called Ecclesiasticks.

Neither is it of any moment that Priests are mentioned to have been or belonged to this Order, because it is not denyed that under the general Designation of Templars were comprehended the Priests, who peculiarly served that Order, and had Benefices, as in *Scotland,* the Ministers of the four Churches of *Tulloch* and *Aboyne, Inchennan,* and *Maryculter ;* Which Priests belonging to the Order by *Eugen* the 3d were allowed to wear the reid Cross of the Order, but that will not make the Order it self, and the Revenues belonging to it ecclesiastick ; For *Eugen* the 3d does expresly distinguish betwixt the Priests and the Order, and under the general Designation of Templars, there were 3 several Classes, *viz.* The Knights, the *fratres minores* or *servientes,* and Priests or Chaplands belonging to the Order, whereof the first two were secular, and as to the Knights it is acknowledged by Lawyers, *quod milites seu æquites crucifieri seorsim & seculariter vivebant & sæpe uxorati.*

As to the great account of the original of this Order, it is in general to be observed, that the Order of the Templar, the Hospitulars, the Tutonick Order, and some orders of *Spain* were institute much about the same time, and in all these Orders the Church did impose upon the Princes and great Men of Christendome, as they did in the whole project of the *Croisads* for recovering the Holy Land, and for that end these orders were institute and preached up ; And for the more specious pretext, all of them had Mixtures and Resemblances of Religion and Vowes, whereof the remains are yet to be seen in the Habits and Crosses of the several Orders of Christendome, and particularly of the Garter, which has a Dean, 12 Cannons, besides petty Cannons, and had 26 poor Kights, whose Maintenance is settled upon them for their praying for the Order ; As also they had St. *George* for their Patron, and had a Prelate Chancellor and Register all Clergie men, and yet this neither is nor ever was reckoned a religious Order.

But to come closser to the Knights Templars, it is apparent that they had their first Establishment from *Baldwine* King of *Jerusalem,* and albeit they made their first Vowes in the hands of their Patriarch, as Vowes in these days used to be made in the
hands

hands of Church men, yet they were not for that Ecclesiastick, that being done only for the more solemnity of their Vowes, and obtaining the Patriarchs Benediction, and it is observable, that they were several years institute before they were confirmed by the Council of *Troyas*, neither were they confirmed in *Italy*, till the time of *Innocent* the *3d.* in the year 1198, and it was no Mervel that the Popes did interpose in that matter, and were proud to have them called their Sons and Subjects, Titles which the greatest Monarchs bore; For indeed they were as *St. Bernard* calls them a new kind of Militia, and they were extreamly fitted for the Ambition of the Popes, for subjecting the temporal powers of Christendome to the holy See, in conjunction with the numerous progeny of other Orders; And therefore the Popes did look upon themselves as particularly concerned in the protection of the Templars, till they became too great and to interfier with the Clergie and Church it self, yet they were no more Ecclesiastick than the Popes Guards, or than the other Princes who were ingadged in the holy War, or even the Souldiers who all undertook a design of the same kind, and wore the Badge of the Reid-Cross, and who received from the Pope their reid Standard *in anno* 1095, or 1096, under *Urban* the *2d.*

Nor is the judgement of the Colledge of *Paris* of any importance in this case, for there is no doubt of this Order having as has been said a resemblance of religious Orders, did plead an exemption from the secular Jurisdiction, and even from the ordinary Jurisdiction of the Church, and were only subject to the great Master, and to his Laws and Constitutions Likeas the Benefices which they injoyed were conferred by the great Master *pleno jure tanquam habens amni modam potestatem*, and he dispensed with their Vowes; And it is to be observed, that the Doctors of *Sorbon* do not call the Templars religious, but only say they ought to pass amongst the religious, and enjoy the benefit of Exemption, because they have listed themselves for the defence of Faith, and have made profession of the Religion established by the Church, and the Doctors who generally allow them *privilegium fori*, are very far from granting that they were a religious Order, or were *religiosi*, as may appear from *Charlavalius* in the forecited place: This Exemption or *privilegium fori* was the effect of their own greatness, and the indulgence

of

of the Church of *Rome* for her own ends, but did not alter the design or Character of the Order from Secular to Ecclesiastick.

And as to what is contained in the Resolves of the Doctors of *Paris*, concerning the Goods of the Templars, *viz.* That their Goods should be applyed to the ends for which at first they were conferred upon them : It does not determine whether the Goods were Ecclesiastick or not, but the haill Resolve was a Cheque upon the impetuous Avarice and Revenge of *Philip* the *Fair*.

As to the extraordinary Power the Pope did arrogat to himself in the Tryal, Suppression and Disposal of the Goods of the Templars; It will amount to no Argument with any that are in the least conversant in the Historie of these times, wherein there was nothing Civil exempted from the ambitious pretensions of these Pontifices, and yet in this Matter the Pope proceeded by his own Confession, without observing the Forms of Law or Justice. And farder, it appears from the Bulls in *July* 1308, That the Application of the Lands belonging to the Templars was qualified so as not to prejudice the Right of the Kings and other Lords; Which Quality the Pope again owns in his Letter to the *French* King.

After all, this Decree did never take fully effect, for although the Templars were generally supprest, yet their Goods were scarce united to the Hospitulars any where without paying of great Sums. In *Arrogan* and *Castile*, their Possessions were transferred to the Knights of *Callatrava*, and many of their Possessions were retained by the Knights themselves. In *Portugal* their Lands were united to a new Order of Knighthood then erected; So that the Decree of this Council was never universally and fully received. This effect indeed it had, That the *French* King who conceived a Jealousie at the Templars for their Greatness, and to whom they were suspected as concerning Tumults that arose concerning his debasing the Coyn : He was revenged by their Suppression, and secured against their Fears, and inriched by the Money extorted from the Hospitulars on pretence of giving them their Lands; And the Pope at the same time got the disposal of vast Estates belonging to them, rid himself of an Order which was become formidable, and which above all made *Philip* the *Fair* submit to have *Boniface* the 8th *Clement's* Predicessor voted a good Catholick in the same Council of *Vienn*, which condemned and suppressed the Templars,

albeit

albeit in several Provincial and National Synods and Councils they had been absolved.

From the whole it is apparent, 1. That the Templars were several years institute before they were Confirmed, or received any Habit, Rule, or Confirmation, by any Council acknowledged by the Church of *Rome*. 2. That the Design of their institution was the guarding of the High Roads going or coming to the Holy Sepulchar, and that by Force of Arms, which is incompatible with the Essential Character of Religious Orders, according to the Cannonist; These Orders being always institute for some Spiritual Perfection, and consequently the Revenues bestowed upon these Knights were not Ecclesiastick, and to this may be applyed very fitly the words of the said *Tholousanus*, Lib. 15. Cap. 23. Numb. 19. speaking of the *Præbendæ*, says, *Alterius generis Præbendæ quæ debenter clericis spirituales dicuntur & beneficii ecclesiasticæ nomine censentur quod habeant spirituale munus annexum.* And indeed the distinguishing Character of the Ecclesiastick Benefice was, That they had *spirituale munus annexum*, for which *Tholousanus* cites his authority. 3. Albeit the Church did afterwards confirm the Order which was so much for their Profit and Interest, and that there were Exemptions added for their greater Dignity, yet that did not change the Nature of the Order from Militarie to Religious, as the Church of *Rome* was pleased to call all the Orders of her Devotars; But because of these Exemtions, the Benefices belonging to these Militarie Orders were considered as *beneficia habentia finitatem cum beneficiis ecclesiasticis.* Tholousanus *in tractatu: de beneficiis ecclesiasticis,* Cap. 9. Numb. 11. Says, *Præceptoriæ dictæ commendæ sacrorum militum non proprie dicentur ex genere beneficiorum eo quod personæ conferentes & quibus conferuntur non sint* Laici *nec ecclesiasticæ sed tertiæ ordinis.* 4. That long before the Reformation, *viz.* in the 1312, this Order was supprest, and the very Cause of the Institution, which was the guarding of the Holy Sepulchar had failled, the Christians being beat out of the Holy Land about the end of the 13*th* Centurie, and the Cheats of the Croisads being too gross to pass longer upon the European World, and albeit the Knights Hospitulars did continue longer in repute, yet even their Credit and Interest decayed after these vain designs were over, except in such places in *Europe*

as

as were almost continually ingaged in War against the *Turks*, and their Revenues were injoyed in a way almost hereditary, especially in *Scotland*, which is observable from Sir *James Sandilands* Charter, bearing that the Preceptory had belonged to him and his Predecessors for some time past, or as the Charter bears *quibusque temporibus retro actus.* 5. That upon the Suppression of the Templars their Revenues which were never Ecclesiastick fell to the Fisk, as *bona vacantia,* and were generally seased by the secular Powers, as is observed by *Spanheim* in his *seculo* 14. *cap.* 8. *in fine. Ita quemadmodum in* Callia, *similiter & in aliis Nationibus quem iibet principem eorum quæ in suo dominio reperit, si non omnia tamen plurima suis usibus & fisco applicasse una vox est historicorum.*

And albeit the Pope and the Councill of the *Vienn* did in appearance suppress the Order, and apply the Revenues to the Hospitulars or Knights of *St. John*, yet it is manifest that the Popes did proceed in that matter, not by the way of Law, which if the Templars had been an ecclesiastick Order, the Pope and Council would never have confest, for it is but too well known with how much Arrogancy they pretend to dispose of the ecclesiastick Orders, and their Revenues, by their proper Authority of altering, uniting, disjoyning, or transferring of Benefices, but the Pope did in this matter proceed truly by way of intrigue, and the Authority of the Council was added for the better oppression of the Templars, wherein the Princes did concur for their own particular ends, having begun to wearie of the Holy War; And it is observed by *Massonious, Templarios si respicimus ad impiam accusationem, aulicorum persuasiones & spem lucri & in sortium supplicia & eversionis modum fuisse injuria eversos regen certe impium pontificem implementem nec mitiorem sententiam dicere posse lectores.*

And as these were the circumstances of the Templars, at, and before their Suppression in forreign Countries, so that it is certain, the Templars, nor even the Hospitulars, were not with us reckoned an Ecclesiastick Order, but Militar and Secular, and in a M. S. remains supposed to be of Sir *John Nisbet's;* He observes that in solemn Processions, or Meetings of Parliaments, or Conventions, the Preceptors, or these Orders, were ranked with the Laity, neither did they bear Burdens of Taxes with the Clergy, or pay any

part

part of their Contributions, but with the Laity, nor were their Lands comprehended within the Acts concerning the Assumption of the Thirds of Benefices ; So that it is evident in this Kingdom, they were all reckoned as Secular, as indeed they were: And albeit they had Churches, whereof they were properly Patrons, and to which Churches my Lord *Torphichen* pays yet a considerable Stipend, yet that did not make them Ecclesiastick, as has been above said.

The clear and precise answer to the Defence is, 1. Neither were the Templars Ecclesiastick, neither were their Possessions Church Benefices, and therefore fell not under the Act of Annexation. 2. *Esto* they had been originally Church-benefices, yet the Order being supprest 200 years before the Reformation, the Act of Annexation which was visibly made upon that occasion, does not comprehend the Temple-lands, or even the possession of the Knights Hospitulars, which were devolved upon the Crown long before the Reformation, and not upon the general account of Reforming the Errors of the Church of *Rome*, but because the end for which these Military Orders were instituted, the intertaining and gairding of Pilgrims at *Jerusalem* was long before ceassed, and the *Croisads* were abandoned. 3. If these Temple lands did fall under the Act of Annexation, then they were again excepted from it expresly in a Clause concerning the Lands and Lordship of *Torphichen*, and which Clause was not taken away by the general Act 1633, because *illud non agebatur* to take away the special Exceptions, but the general Act did extend the Annexation 1587, which did only concern the Benefices, which at the date of that Act the 29 *July* the said year, were in the possession of Church-men into the Right and Superiority of all Lands, Baronies erected before or after the Act of Annexation 1587, which only concerned the general Reservations contained in the Act 1587, it was never rescinded, and these Reservations being in a solemn Act full 40 years before the 1633, was so clearly established upon the Authority of Law and Right, that unless they had been expressly rescinded, they must yet subsist, and the extension of the Act as to the general case will not cut of the special Priviledges. 4. Neither does the general Clause in the Act of Parliament 1633 extend to the Temple lands, for albeit it mentions the Superiorities belonging to whatsomever Abbacies, Priories, Prioresses,

oresses, Preceptories, yet that is to be taken in a proper sense, and the Commendams or Preceptories belonging to the Military Orders were not properly Benefices and only a Resemblance of them; But for an evidence that these Acts did only concern the Benefices which belong to Churches, Abbacies, Convents or Hospitals; The Lords would be pleased to observe that the narrative of the Act 1587, mentions, *That our Soveraign Lord perfectly understanding that the greatest part of his propper Rent had been given away to Abbacies, Monastries, and other persons of Clergy, and seing the Causes of the Dissolution of the Patrimony of the Crown to the Church, after the Truth knawing, are found neither necessary nor profitable, it is found meet and expedient that the King should have recourse to his own Patrimony; Therefore his Majesty and the Estates unites to the Crown all Lands,* &c. which at that day the 29 July 1587, *pertained to Archbishops, Bishops, Abbots, Priors, Prioresses or other Prelate, Ecclesiastick or beneficed Persons of whatsomever Estate, and what pertained to Abbayces, Convents and Cloysters, of whatever order of Friars, Nuns, Monks or Channons.* And the Act 1633 albeit it adds the word *Preceptories,* yet is manifestly relative to the Act 1587 and concerns only the very same subject, with this extension only, that whereas the Act 1587 was confined to the Benefices, which at that time was in the possession of Church men, the Act 1633 did annex, all Lordships erected before that Act or after, and the word *Preceptories* doe   *   *   *   *†

† A few lines have been lost, owing to the unskilfulness of the Binder, in cutting the bottom leaves of the folio volume, in which the original (the only copy known) was preserved. Lord Fountainhall has given the details of this curious dispute, *Decisions,* vol. ii. p. 94.

The result was favourable to the Temple Superior. The Information for the Vassals is unfortunately not to be found.

INFORMATION

For JOHN LORD TORPHICHEN, to be presented to the Lords Commissioners appointed by his Majesty for the Trial of the rights and securities of the Kirklands, Abbacies, Priories, and other Ecclesiastical Benefices erected by his Majesty's Predecessors *in temporalibus*, for consideration of the original and fundamental grounds whereupon the same hath proceeded.

IT is Represented, that the antient and honourable military Order of the Knights of the Hospital of St. John of Hyerusalem, and Temple of Salomon, had its beginning, about the time of Godfrey of Bouillion. Some deuote Gentlemen coming to uisite Hyerusalem, and having built an Hospital, which was the first abode of the Knights, called from thence Hospitaliers, this martial order was approved by the common consent of Christian Princes. The Duty of their profession, in the beginning, was to receive the Christians that came from all parts, to visit the holy land, to assist them on their way, and to secure them against the Arabians and other Infidels. Pope Calixtus and Paschal allowed this order, and never arrogated any authority over the Knights, further, than their universal authority *ver* all other Secular Estates.

By the ancient Statutes, composed by Raymond de Podio, Great Master of the Hospital, the Knights who were to be admitted, were to be Gentlemen of Name and Arms, of noble descent and extraction, not indebted in great sums of money, not bastards, nor married.

NOTA.—Archibaldus Magister de Torphiphen, is witness to a charter of Alexander Grand Steward of Scotland, anno 1252.

ried. They promised at their entry, to enjoy nothing in proper, neither in lands nor goods. They vowed obedience to their Superiour, and to defend and advance at their power the Catholick Roman Religion. There was never any considerable Enterprise, *in Bello sacro*, against the Infidels, where they were not actors ; which services gained them the singular favour of Christian Princes, and religious subjects, who bestowed liberally on the order, large and ample Rents and Revenues.

MALCOLM King of Scotland, ' In liberam et puram Elymosynam, ' donavit Fratribus Hospitalis Hyerosolimitani, Militibus Templi ' Solomonis unum plenarium Toftum in quolibet Burgo, totius ' terræ suæ.' This foundation was enlarged by succeeding Kings, especially by Alexander I. II. and III. Robert the II. James the II. III. and IV. Kings of Scotland. Their Successors, did not only confirm the precedent donations, but by new Dispositions, of certain Lands and Territories, indued with diuers priuilegis and immunities, and the right of patronage of some Churches, made up an temporal rent and revenue, called the Lordship of St. John, and Preceptorie of Torphiphin, largely amplified by the subjects, by some parts of their own inheritance, now lyand dispersed through the haill parisches and sherifdomes of the Kingdom, commonly called TERRÆ TEMPLARIÆ, *quasi Terræ concessæ Militibus Templi Solomonis.*

This Lordship or Preceptorie, founded, as said is, to the Hospital of St. John of Hierusalem, was always conferred by the Great Master thereof, with Consent of the Convent and Knights, to an noble and martial man, lawfully begotten, and born within the Kingdom ; and it was granted to the present Præceptor, to make choice of a worthy Gentleman to succeed him in his place and state.—So in the days of K. James the III,—

1. Sir Gualtur Dundas, then Præceptor, elected and
2. directed Sir William Knowes to Rhodes, to give proue of his sufficiency ; who thereafter was receivit and admittit to the place, and in end became a great Counsellour and Thesaurer to K. James IV.
3. Sir William Knowes, did nominat and recommend to the Great Master,

NOTA.—Willielmus Knolius Præceptor de Torphiphen, is witness to King James IV. his Charter at Perth, without any other designation, anno 1470.

Master, Sir Walter Lindsay, his successour, a valiant Gentleman, oftentimes imployed by King James V. against the English, who discharged his Trust with great Commendation.

4. Sir Walter, in his time, maid choice of Sir James Sandielandis, whom he recommended to the Great Master of the Order, then resident at Malta; who after his abode there, by the space of two yeiris compleit, in consideration of his worth and sufficiency, he was created futur successour to Sir Walter, by the Great Master, and the Council of his Knights, as his Patent plainly imports, and the prouision and donation thereof, was gifted be them, *pleno jure, quasi plenariam habentes potestatem donandi,* as the terms of the Donation and Admission proports.

This form of Presentation and Admission of the Præceptor of Torphephin continued many ages, till the days of Mary Queen of Scotland, and all this time, the Præceptors thereof, in Parliament and General Councils, were ranked amongst the Nobles, and placed upon the TEMPORAL side.—*Inter proceres, habebant jus suffragij,* since K. James III. as the extract of the Parliament Rolls since that time, under the Clerk Register his hands, doth justify clearly.

At the Reformation, the Pope's authority and jurisdiction, being found by the Estates to be prejudicial to the supreme authority of the Prince, therefore, by Act of Parliament 1560, it was enacted, That no subject should have recourse to his See, nor any of his Profession, under pain of forfaulture and banishment; and never to enjoy any Honour, Office or Dignity within the Realm: and this Statute being ordained by subsequent Acts of Parliament, as a perpetual Law to all the Leiges in all time coming, whereby the original foundation and mortification of the Preceptorie of Torphephen, *Fratribus Hospitalis Hierosolimitani, Militibus Templi Solomonis,* was abrogate and cancell'd, in so far as the principal cause and reason of the foundation, was the service enjoined to the Præceptor, upon oath, to defend and advance the Roman Catholick Religion, which Romish Religion, by an established Law, is declared to be prejudiciable to Royal authority, and hurtful to the kingdom; and therefore the authority of the Bishop of Rome, and all other of his Sect, utterly abolished and simply discharged, whereby the
power

NOTA.—Sir Henry Levingston, of the Family of Kylsyth, in Stirlingshire, is stiled by Crawfurd, p. 240. Præceptor of Torphiphen.

power and prerogative of the Great Master, and the foresaid Knights, in ordaining and creating the said Preceptors, was extinct and annulled, and all their right dissolved from them and their order, and devolved to the Crown, *Jure devoluto*, by the established Law aforsaid, and so vested, *in arbitrio Principis, sede vacante,* to dispone thereupon at his pleasure, in all time coming.

About which time, Sir James Sandilands, Lord St. John, lawful Titular and Possesor of the Lordship, who had entered young into the service at the Court of K. James V. and thereafter, was domestick servant to Queen Mary Regent, create and constitute Master Usher of her Majesty's House and Chamber, and after her decease, continued his service, place and credit, with Queen Mary, her daughter, who, after trial of his worth and sufficiency, was employed by her Majesty, in diverse weighty affairs, and at two or three several times, chosen ambassador to divers foreign princes.

This Nobleman at this time, in regard of the great alteration fallen furth in the Kingdom, with advise of the wisest Lawyers of that time, in respect of the forsaid Acts, the full title and right of the said Preceptorie, whensoever it should vack, falling to the Crown, to remain with her Masjesty, as a part of his property and patrimony, *attento maxime,* that no Successour could never be lawfully provided to that place, was encouraged to present to her Majesty his humble Petition, That it would please her Grace, to sett and dispose to him in feu-farme, his own Preceptorie, for such a competent composition and yearly feu-duty to be paid therfore to her Highness and her Successours, as it should please her Grace and the Lords of her Council and Exchequer to impose thereupon.

It pleased her Grace, calling to mind his long attendance and service to her father, mother and herself, his great Charges and Expences in foreign employment, to grant his Petition and Desire; and for expedition thereof, direct a Signature to that effect, to be compon'd by the Lords of her Council and Exchequer, who by reason of some urgent necessities, dayly occurring in her Highness's affairs, Composed for Ten Thousand Crowns of the Sun, togithir with an yearly feu-duty of five hundred Marks, to be paid to her Highness and her successors for ever.

Which Condition he acceptit, and to the effect he might be infeft, he personally compeirit in presence of the Queen's Majesty, the Lord Chancelour the Earles of Murray, Marischall, and diuers

other

others of her Hienes Privy Council, and ther, as the only lawful undoubted Titular, and present possessor of the Lordship and Preceptorie of Torphephen, which was never subject to any Chapter or Conuent whatsomever, except only the Knights of Jerusalem and Temple of Salomon, *Genibus flexis et reverentia qua decuit,* resigned and ouergaue in the hands of our Souerane Lady, his undoubted Superior, *ad perpetuam remanentiam,* all Right, Property and Possession, which he had, or any way could pretend to the said Preceptorie, or any part thereof, in all time Coming; to the effect the same might remain perpetually, with her Hyeness and her Successours, as a Part of Property and Patrimony of her Crown for ever.

After this Resignation in the Queen's Majesty's hands, *ad Remanentiam,* of this Benefice, be the lawful Titular thereof; her Hyeness, in remembrance of the good service of the said Sir James Sandilands, gave and grantid and dispon'd, in feu-farme, heretably, to the said Sir James, his heirs and assignies, ALL and HAILL, the said Preceptorie and Lordship, *sub hac forma.*

𝔐𝔞𝔯𝔦𝔞 Dei gratia Regina Scotorum omnibus probis hominibus totius terræ suæ Clericis et Laicis salutem. Sciatis nos considerantes fidele, nobile, et gratuitum servitum, nobis, nostrisque patri et matri bonæ memoriæ in reipublicæ et regni nostrum commodum impensum per dilectum nostrum domesticum servitorem Jacobum Sandelandis Dominum de St. Johns, ac recordantes supplicationem per nobilitatem et tres regni nostri status, in ejus gratiam, paulo ante nostram a Francia in hoc nostrum regnum perfectionem nobis directarum quarum in ultimo nostro Parliamento apud Edinburgh, quarto die mensis Junii ultime elapsi, tento, minime obliviscentes, easdem ad nobilitatis et trium ordinum præscriptorum memoriam reduximus, in pleno Parliamento proprio ore declarando nobis fore gratum, quod dicti nostri regni status et ejusdem nobilitas, dictum nostrum servitorem tanta æstimatione dignum arbitrarentur, ac quod a nobis tanti æstimaretur; cujus servitii respectu ac supplicationum præscriptarum animum gratum ac nostrum erga ipsum favorem declarare præmisimus, cui rei nostre status gratanter assentierunt, Nos propterea, ac pro augmentatione Patrimonii coronæ nostræ annuatim in summam quingentarum Marcarum pro terris subscriptis, de quibus nos, nec nostri Prædecessores, nullum ante hoc commodum

retulimus,

retulimus, necnon pro summa decem mille scutorum aureorum so-larum vulgari appellatione crownes of the Sun nuncupat, dedimus et concessimus hæreditarie dicto Domino Jacobo, hæredibus suis et assignatis, &c. &c.

The words Dispositive of the Infeftment, containe the Baronie of Torphephen, Liston, Balintrodo, Mare Culter, Dennie, Than-kertoun and Galtua, with the right of Patronage of some Kirkes and some Teyndis, possesst in property by the said Præceptor and his predecessors, not particularly designed ; Togither also with an ample privilege of Regality. The *reddendo*, bears five hunderid Marks feu-diuty, yearly and termly ; and for the right of Patron-age of the said Churches and Teyndis foirsaid, he is obliged be an special prouision, Sub hac forma. ' Et pro præfatis Decimis, ' Tenendo et sustentando, infra Ecclesias dictæ Præceptoriæ, per-' prius spectantes, habiles et idoneos Ministros, prout ordo pro ' presenti, seu postea, communiter infra regnum nostrum erit ma-' gis usitatus.'
It is to be noted, that there is no later Act of Parliament, nor other Law, nor supervenient Right, after the forsaid Act 1560, whereby the King can pretend any title or entry to the Præceptory : —That the said Act 1560, was Ratified by K. James his first Par-liament and Second Chapter, and decerned to remain a perpetual law to all his Subjects in time coming, that the Queen's Majesty at the time might set in feu-ferme, without diminution of her Rental, any part of her property, by the Acts of Parliament of James the II. Parliament 14. Chap. 72.—James the IV. Parl. 6. Chap. 90—James the V. Parl. 7. Chap. 116.—James the VI. Parl. 14. Chap. 204.—James the VI. Parl. 11. Chap. 30.—And so the new Infeft-ment of this Preceptory is lawful and valid, specially, seeing it is granted *Titulo oneroso*, for a Composition of a great sum of money, really paid ; and for the feu-duty of five hundred Marks yearly, to be payd to her Highness, and her successors for ever, whereas she nor her predecessors never received any benefit out of the said Pre-ceptory before, any manner of way.
That this Benefice was never annexit to the Crown, and is ex-pressly exceptit in the Act of Annexation of K. James VI. Parl. 11. cap. 29. and decerned to remaine to the Feuar thereof and Ti-tular, after the forme and tenour of the Infeftment in al time coming.

ing. That albeit the Charter bearis present payment of ten thousand crownis, that the money was paid at diverse times, partly upon her Majestys precepts to her servents, french Paris, Sir Robert Meluin, Sir James Balfour and Captain Anstruther, and the rest of the soume to Mr Robert Richardson, Thresaurer for the time, whereof there is a receipt under the Privy Seal.

That a great part of that money, numerat in Gold and Silver, was borrowed from Timothy Curneoli, an Italian Gentleman of the Preceptor's acquaintance, at Genoa, and a Banquier of the house of * , resident in Scotland for the time.

That the Nobilman, being burdenit with great depts, for his exoneration and reliff, was forced to let in feu to his Tennands, their own Roumes, for a reasonable Composition, binding himself and his heiris, to warrand them, *contra omnes et mortales*.

That the greatest part of his Lordship's Estate, viz. the Barony of Marie Culter, the Barony of Denny, the Barony of Thankertoun, the Barony of Galtua, and the most part of the Barony of Balintrodo, were resigned to the hands of K. James, by the unquhil Sir James of Sandelands, and the vassals thereof, obliged to pay to his Majesty, the feu-duties of the same, yearly and termly; so at the time of the Information, there remained only in the hands of the Lord Torphephin, the superiority of the thretty pund Land of the Barony of Torphephin, and the Thretty pund Land of the Barony of Liston. John Earle of Marr, heretable feuar and proprietor of the principal messuage thereof, which he holds of our souerain Lord the King, immediatly, paying to his Hieness Exchequer, the few-mailis and duties thereof.

That the present Estate of the Churches, proper to the Lordship, which are only Four in number, with the viccarage of the Church of Marie-Culter, the Kirks of Tullaich and Oboyne, the Kirk of Inchinnen, and the Kirk of Torphephin;—Tullaich and Oboyne, twa Kirks in the North, situat in the Highlands, and Scherifdom of Aberdene, the parisches whereof are little in quantity, and very bad in quality, the teyndis and deuties thereof are disponed by my Lord Torphephin, for sustentation of the Minister who serves the Cure, without reservation of any part thereof to himself.

The

* Blank in the original.

The Kirk of Inchinnen, within the sherifdome of Renfrew, having belonged for several ages, to the Earles of Lennox, and at present possest by the Duke of Lennox his taksmen, for several yeares, is disponed and assigned, and disposed by my Lord Torphephin, to the Minister serving the Cure.

The Kirk of Torphephin, with the Sherifdome of Linlithgou, the one half thereof, consisting of the Thretty pund lands of the Barony of Torphephin, belonging to my Lord in property and superiority, *cum decimis ejusdem inclusis, nunquam a stipite seperari solitis;* The Rental bou extending yearly, to Seven Chalder victual; The other half of the Parish, being possest, by divers Titulars and proprietors, the Rental bous of the same, extending to other Seven Chalders victual yearly, whereof five chalders are disponed yearly, by my Lord, to the Minister deserving the Cure, with the vicarage of the Kirk.

That the vicarage of the Kirk of Mary Culter, not being sufficient to sustain the Minister serving the Cure, the great Teinds thereof, being hailly possest by other Titulars, my Lord Torphephen, hath bund himself and his heirs, to pay to the said Minister, yearlie, the soume of fifty marks, out of his own proper rent and patrimony.

This being the treu account, of the only Military Benefice within this Kingdom, founded by the Beneficence of divers of our Princes and Kings, and largely endowed by the voluntar donations of the subjects, mortified to the Hospital and Knights of Hierusalem, for the entertainment and maintenance of the honourable estate of an Knight of the Order, within this Kingdom; Sir John Sandelands, as retoured and served heir to his predecessor, and to the Lordship of Torphephen, Represents, that as his Benefice differs in nature, quality, circumstances, from all the other infeftments of erections, within the Realm, called in question at the time; being the only erection in Q. Mary's time, so that it may be tried by itself, and his Petition accordingly answered.*

* Printed from a copy preserved amongst the Macfarlane MSS. in the Advocates' Library: *Diplomata,* vol. ii. p. 461. The notes are by Macfarlane. It is remarkable, that " Torphephin" or " Torphiphen" has been uniformly used, instead of the proper word " Torphichen."

Templaria.

PART II.

MDCCCXXVIII.

TWENTY-FIVE COPIES PRINTED.

CHARTER

GRANTED BY KING JAMES IV. OF SCOTLAND,

IN FAVOUR OF

THE KNIGHTS HOSPITALLERS;

CONFIRMING ANCIENT ROYAL GRANTS BY KINGS
MALCOLM IV. ALEXANDER II. ALEXANDER III.
JAMES II. AND JAMES III.

IACOBUS Dei gracia rex Scotorum OMNIBUS probis hominibus tocius terre sue clericis et laicis salutem SCIATIS nos quasdam cartas et euidencias per quondam nostros illustrissimos predecessores Scotorum reges factas et concessas Deo et SANCTO HOS-
PITALI DE IERUSALEM ET FRATRIBUS EIUSDEM MILITIE TEM-
PLI SALAMONIS videlicet CARTAM confirmacionis quondam
serenissimi patris nostri[1] cuius anime propicietur Deus factam super
Carta confirmacionis quondam aui nostri Iacobi secundi regis Scotorum in qua inseruntur quatuor Carte quondam predecessorum
nostrorum Malcolmi[2] et Alexandri[3] Scotorum regum facte dicto
Hospitali de Ierusalem nunc Torfiching nuncupat. ac ffratribus eiusdem de nonnullis elemosinis terris toftis libertatibus tholoneis consuetudinibus in empcionibus et vendicionibus qualitercunque contingen. amerciamentis et priuilegiis ac super feodo et forisfactura
suorum libere tenencium ut in dictis quatuor cartis predecessorum
nostrorum in eisdem cartis confirmacionis in forma maiori insertis
plenius constat et continetur de mandato nostro uisam lectam inspectam diligenter examinatam sanam integram non rasam non cancellatam nec in aliqua sua parte suspectam ad plenum intellexisse
sub

sub hac forma   (I.) IACOBUS[4] Dei gracia rex Scotorum   Omnibus
probis hominibus tocius terre sue clericis et laicis salutem   Sciatis
nos quasdam cartas et euidencias per nostros illustrissimos predecessores factas et concessas Deo et sancto Hospitali de Ierusalem ffratribus
eiusdem militie Templi Salamonis videlicet Cartam confirmacionis
quondam nostri serenissimi progenitoris Iacobi secundi Scotorum
regis factam super cartis quondam Malcolmi et Alexandri Scotorum
regum dicto Hospitali de Ierusalem nunc Torfichin nuncupato ac
ffratribus eiusdem de nonnullis elemosinis terris toftis libertatibus
tholoneis consuetudinibus in empcionibus et vendicionibus et qualitercunque contingen. amerciamentis et priuilegiis vt in quatuor
cartis predicessorum nostrorum in dicta carta confirmacionis in
maiori forma insertis continetur de mandato nostro uisam lectam
inspectam et diligenter examinatam sanam integram non rasam non
cancellatam nec in aliqua sui parte suspectam ad plenum intellexisse
sub hac forma   (II.) IACOBUS[5] Dei gratia rex Scotorum   Omnibus
probis hominibus tocius terre nostre clericis et laicis salutem   Sciatis nos uidisse inspexisse et diligenter examinasse cartas et euidencias illustrissimorum progenitorum et antecessorum nostrorum, viz.
Malcolmi Alexandri et Alexandri regum Scocie quarum tenores
de verbo in uerbum sequuntur   (III.) MALCOLMUS[6] rex Scotorum
episcopis abbatibus prioribus comitibus baronibus Justiciariis, vicecomitibus prepositis ministris et omnibus probis (hominibus) tocius
sue terre tam futuris quam presentibus salutem   Sciatis me concessisse et dedisse et hac presenti carta mea confirmasse Deo et
Sancto Hospitali de Ierusalem vnum plenarium toftum in quolibet
meo burgo tocius mee terre pro Dei amore et pro salute antecessorum meorum et pro mea salute ad tenend. ita bene et libere vt ipsi
tenent suas alias elemosinas sicut elemosine libere tenere debent.
T.[7] Sonsan episcopo de Brechin Waltero cancellario Gospatricio
comite W.[8] filio Alani Wilelmo Carpentario Apud Brechin[9]
(IV.) ALEXANDER[10] Dei gracia rex Scotorum Omnibus probis
hominibus tocius terre sue clericis et laicis salutem. Sciatis presentes
et futuri nos concessisse et hac carta nostra confirmasse Deo et ffratribus Hospitalis Ierusalem omnes donaciones terrarum et hospitalium
et elemosinarum que eis racionabiliter facte sunt tam in ecclesiis
quam in aliis rebus et possessionibus mundanis Volumus eciam et
firmiter precipimus vt predicti ffratres omnes possessiones et elimosi-
nas suas habeant et teneant adeo libere et quiete sicut carta clare
memorie

memorie domini regis Alexandri[11] patris nostri super hiis et aliis libertatibus dictis ffratribus confecta proportat et testatur Volumus eciam et concedimus omnibus hominibus predictorum ffratrum et qui de eisdem quicquid tenent in burgo aut extra burgum vt quieti sint ab omni tholoneo et ab omnibus aliis consuetudinibus in omnibus empcionibus et vendicionibus mundanis qualitercunque contingen. Et si coram nobis uel aliquibus balliuis nostris super aliquo defectu fuerint amerciati prefata amerciamenta Sancto Iohanni et dictis fratribus concessimus imperpetuum Et si idem ffratres aliquomodo fuerint amerciati sint quieti pro vna vlna albi scarleti Volumus insuper et concedimus vt dicti ffratres omnia prescripta habeant et teneant in liberam puram et perpetuam elimosinam Testibus Malis comite de Stratherne Donaldo comite de Mar Iacobo senescallo Scocie Apud Scone decimo septimo die mensis Iunii anno regni nostri tricesimo quinto[12] (V.) ALEXANDER[13] Dei gracia rex Scotorum Omnibus probis hominibus tocius terre sue clericis et laicis salutem Sciant presentes et futuri nos concessisse Deo et ffratribus Hospitalis Ierusalem omnes donaciones terrarum hominum et tenencium ac elemosinarum que eis racionabiliter facte sunt tam in ecclesiis quam in aliis rebus priuilegiis et possessionibus mundanis Volumus igitur et precipimus vt dicti ffratres omnes possessiones et elemosinas suas habeant et teneant cum sok et sak thol et theme infang-theiff et cum omnibus aliis hereditatibus et liberis consuetudinibus suis in bosco et plano in pratis et pascuis in aquis et molendinis in viis et semitis in moris et marressiis in stagnis et viuariis in piscariis in grangiis ac virgultis infra burgum et extra et in omnibus rebus liberis et quietis de placitis et querelis scutagio auxilio et assisis et de operatione castellorum et poncium et de bludewitis et de passagio pontagio et hospilagio et quieti de omni tholoneo et de omni seculari seruicio opere seruili exaccione et de omnibus aliis consuetudinibus secularibus excepta solum hominis iusticia condempnati exceptis quatuor querelis que ad coronam nostram pertinent scilicet de rapina de combustione de murthir et de femina efforciata Volumus et concedimus omnibus hominibus predictorum ffratrum et eisdem tenentes quicquid in burgo uel extra burgum ut liberi ab omni tholoneo et de omnibus aliis consuetudinibus in omnibus empcionibus et vendicionibus qualitercunque contingen. Volumus insuper et firmiter precipimus ut si homines eorundem ffratrum et tenentes coram nobis uel aliquibus balliuis nostris pro aliqua

aliqua fuerint amerciati prefata amerciamenta Sancto Iohanni et predictis ffratribus remaneant imperpetuum Et si predicte ffratres aliquomodo fuerint amerciati sint quieti pro una virga scarleti Quare volumus et concedimus et firmiter precipimus ut si predicti ffratres omnia prescripta habeant uel capeant teneant de nobis et successoribus nostris in liberam puram et perpetuam elimosinam secundum quod liberius et quiecius ac plenius temporibus antecessorum nostrorum et successorum nostrorum Regum Scotorum illustrium habere consueuerunt Hec autem omnia prescripta damus concedimus et confirmamus pro amore Dei et animabus omnium antecessorum et successorum nostrorum Testibus Wilelmo episcopo Glasguen. Andrea episcopo Morauien. Wilelmo de Lindissay tunc cancellario Iohanne comite de Huntyntoune Dauid de Lindsay Ricardo de Campaner Dauid Mariscalli Waltero de Bissate Johanne de Hay Alexandro Streuillis cum multis aliis Apud Castrum puellarum[14] ultimo die mensis Iunij anno regn inostri decimo septimo[15] (VI.) ALEXANDER[16] Dei gracia rex Scotorum episcopis abbatibus prioribus comitibus baronibus Iusticiariis vicecomitibus ministris et omnibus balliuis et fidelibus suis salutem Noueritis nos concessisse et confirmasse Deo et beate Marie et ffratribus Militis Templi Salomonis omnes donaciones terrarum hominum et elemosinarum eis a predecessoribus nostris uel ab aliis in preterito uel in futuro, uel a nobis in presenti Collatas, uel in futuro a regibus uel ab aliorum libertate conferendas, uel alio modo acquisitas uel acquirendas tam in ecclesiis quam in rebus, et possessionibus mundanis Quare volumus et firmiter precipimus quod predicti ffratres et eorum homines possessiones et elemosinas suas habeant et teneant cum omnibus libertatibus et liberis consuetudinibus et quietanciis suis in bosco et plano in pratis et pasturis in aquis in molendinis in viis et semitis in stagnis et viuariis in marresiis et piscariis in grangiis et virgultis infra burgum et extra cum secta sacca thol et theme cum infang-theif et outfang-theif girth-brekin et bludwite flein-girth et murthur latrociis et forcement infra tempus et extra tempus et in omnibus locis et cum omnibus causis que sunt uel esse possunt Concedimus eciam imperpetuum quod predicti ffratres et eorum homines quieti sunt de misericordiis et quod ipsi etomnes homines sui liberi sint ab omni scotto et gildo et omnibus auxiliis regum et vicecomitum et omnium ministorum eorum et wappinschaw et exercitibus placitis et querelis warda et

releuio

releuio et de omnibus operibus castellorum parcorum poncium et clausularum et omni cartagio sinagio et nauigio et domuum regularium edificacione et omnimodo operacione Et prohibemus ne bosci eorum ad predicta opera uel aliqua alia ullo modo capiantur Et similiter bladum eorum et hominum suorum ad castella inuenienda non capiantur Volumus eciam quod libere et sufficienter sine qualibet occasione capiant de omnibus boscis domuum suarum et hominum suorum quum voluerunt nec propter hoc in forisfacto uel misericordia ponantur omnes quoque terras suas effecta sua et hominum suorum jam facta et que imposterum fient eis imperpetuum quietabimus de visu forestariorum et de omnibus aliis consuetudinibus. Concedimus insuper eisdem ffratribus et hominibus suis ut de omnibus boscis quos habent in presenti infra metas foreste possunt assartare et colere sine licencia nostrum uel heredum nostrorum uel balliuorum nostrorum ita quod inde in nullo a nobis uel heredibus nostris uel imperpetuum occasionentur Precipimus eciam quod ipsi ffratres Templi et homines sui liberi sint et quieti ab omni tholoneo in omni foro et in omnibus nundinis et in omni transitu poncium viarum et maris per totum regnum nostrum et per omnes terras nostras et omnia mercata sua et hominum suorum sint similiter in predictis locis ab omni tholoneo quieti Concedimus eciam et confirmamus quod si aliquis hominum suorum pro delicto suo vitam uel membra debeat amittere uel fugeret et in judicio stare noluerit uel aliquod delictum fecerit pro quo debeat super catalla sua ubicunque justicia fieri siue in curia nostra siue in alia curia ipsa catalla sint predictorum ffratrum Et licet ipsis ffratribus sine perturbacione vicicomitum et omnium balliuorum nostrorum et aliorum ponere in saisinam de predictis catallis in predictis casibus et aliis quum balliui nostri sciunt si ad nos pertinerent catalla illam in manu nostra sasire possent et debent Et cum aliquis tenendum predictorum ffratrum feodum suum forisfecerit liceat ipsis ffratribus ponere se in saisinam de ipso feodo et ipsum feodum cum pertinenciis suis possedere non obstante quod nos consueuimus feodum fugitivorum et dampnatorum per annum unum et diem possidere Et similiter si aliquis hominum suorum sit in amerciamento ergo nos uel balliuos nostros pro quacunque causa uel delicto uel forisfacto mercie et amerciamenta pecunie sint collecta in una bursa ad scaccarium nostrum portata predictis ffratribus sint ibidem liberata servata regie maiestatis iusticia mortis et membrorum Concedimus

cedimus eciam eis quod licet libertatum suarum contentarum in hac
carta pro temporis diuturnitate ea usi non fuerint quocunque contingen. Nichilominus tamen eadem libertate de cetero utantur sine
aliqua contradictione non obstan. eo quod temporis diuturnitate ea
usi non fuerint sicut predictum est Hec omnia predicta et omnia
alia et singula secularia seruicia et consuetudines que in hoc
scripto non comprehenduntur eis concedimus et confirmamus in perpetuam elimosinam cum omnibus libertatibus et liberis consuetudinibus quas regia maiestas alicuius domui Religionis conferre po-
test pro Dei amore et pro anima domini Dauid regis Scocie et pro
anima domini Wilelmi regis patris nostri et pro animabus antecessorum et successorum nostrorum Et prohibemus super forisfactu-
ram nostram quod nullus eis vel hominibus suis contra hanc Cartam forisfaciat quia ipsos homines et omnes res suas et possessiones suas et hominum suorum in custodiam et specialem protectio-
nem nostram suscepimus Coram Testibus.¹⁷ Apud Striuilin duo-
decimo die mensis Iulii¹⁸ anno regni nostri vicesimo secundo Quas
quidem cartas euidencias et concessiones in omnibus punctis articulis
et priuilegiis approbamus ratificamus et pro nobis et successoribus
nostris ut premissum est confirmamus Mandantes omnibus et singulis justiciariis vicecomitibus burgorum prepositis balliuis et aliis
liegis nostris dictos ffratres et homines suos eis juribus preuile-
giis et concessionibus uti frui et gaudere libere faciant et permit-
tant absque impedimento uel contradictione In cuius rei testimonium presenti carte nostre confirmacionis magnum sigillum nostrum apponi precepimus Testibus¹⁹ domino Wilelmo Crechtoune
consanguineo et cancellario, reverendo in Xpo patribus Wilelmo et
Ioanne custode nostri priuati sigilli et secretario nostro ecclesia-
rum Glasguen. et Dunkelden. episcopis, Wilelmo et Georgio Douglas
et Angusie comitibus consanguineis nostris carissimis Alexandro
de Levingstoune de Calender Johanne Sibbald de Balgony militibus Iacobo de Levingstoune nostre persone custode capitaneo de
Striuilin et Roberto de Levingstoun compotorum nostrorum rotulatore Apud Striuilin septimo die mensis Maij anno domini millesimo quadringentesimo quadragesimo octauo et regni nostri duo-
decimo. Quasquidem cartas euidencias ac donaciones concessiones
priuelegia ceteraque omnia et singula in eisdem contentas in omnibus
suis punctis et articulis condicionibus et modis ac circumstanciis
suis quibuscunque forma pariter et effectu in omnibus et per omnia
approbamus

approbamus ratificamus et pro nobis et successoribus nostris pro perpetuo confirmamus. In cuius rei testimonium presenti carta nostra confirmacionis magnum sigillum nostrum apponi precipimus. Testibus[20] reuerendissimo in Xpo patre Wilelmo archiepiscopo Sancti Andree ac reuerendissimis in Xpo patribus Iacobo episcopo Dunkelden. cancellario nostro Wilelmo electo confirmato Rossen. Georgeo electo Glasguen. dilectis consanguiniis nostris Dauid comite de Craufurde domino Lindissay magistro hospicii nostri George comite de Huntlye domino Gordoun de Badienauche Wilelmo comite Errol domino le Hay constabulario regni nostri Venerabili in Xpo patre Archibaldo abbate Monasterii nostri sancte Crucis de Edinburghe thesaurio nostro Alexandro domino Glammys Iohanne domino Kennedy Wilelmo domino Abernethy in Rothemay Wilelmo domino Borthwic magistro Dauid Levingstoune rectore de Are nostri secreti sigilli custode Archibaldo Quhytelaw archidiacono Laudonie secretario nostro et domino Alexandro Scot clerico nostrorum rotulorum et registri Apud Edinburgh vicesimo primo die mensis Februarii anno domini millesimo quadringentesimo octuagesimo secundo et regni nostri vicesimo tercio. Quasquidem Cartas et euidencias tam dictas cartas confirmacionum quondam patris et aui nostrorum quam easdem quatuor Cartas predictorum predicessorum ac donaciones concessiones libertates priuilegia ceteraque omnia et singula in eisdem contentis in omnibus suis punctis et articulis condicionibus et modis ac circumstanciis suis quibuscunque forma pariter et effectu in omnibus et per omnia ut premissum est approbamus ratificamus et pro nobis et successoribus nostris pro perpetuo confirmamus AC insuper, ubi in dictis cartis non clare constat in illo termino " de tholoneis" nos tamen ob singulares specialesque fauorem amorem et dilectionem quos gerimus ergo dilectum familiarem militem nostrumque consiliarium dilectum Wilelmum Knollis modernum preceptorem eiusdem Loci de Torfichin nostrum thesaurarium Volumus Concessimus et hac presenti carta nostra Concedimus eidem Preceptori et suis successoribus Preceptoribus de Torfiching ut sint liberi a solucione alicuius custume de quibuscunque bonis et mercanciis suis destinandis per eosdem ad partes extra-marinas pro solucione ipsius Preceptoris responsionis que vero responsio extendit ad ducentos ducatos et quod annuatim in nostro sacccario videatur ad quantam summam custume dicta bona se extendunt et tantum eidem Preceptori allocatur.

In

IN cuius rei testimonium, huic presenti carte nostre confirmacionis magnum sigillum apponi precepimus. TESTIBUS ut supra[21] Apud Edinburghe decimo nono die mensis Octobris anno domini millesimo quadringentesimo octuagesimo octauo et regni nostri primo.[22]

---

[1] Jacobus III.   [2] Malcolmus IV.   [3] Alexander III.   [4] Jacobus III.   [5] Jacobus II.   [6] Malcolmus IV.   [7] Testibus.   [8] Wilelmo.   [9] Circa annum 1153.   [10] Alexander III.   [11] Alexander II.   [12] A. D. 1284.   [13] Alexander II.   [14] Edinburgh Castle.   [15] A. D. 1231.   [16] Alexander II.   [17] No witnesses names are inserted.   [18] A. D. 1236.   [19] Cartæ Jacobi II.   [20] Cartæ Jacobi III.

[21] Viz. Roberto episcopo Glasguen., Georgeo episcopo Dunkelden., Johanne priore Sancti Andree secreti sigilli custode, Wilelmo Knollis preceptore de Torfichin thesaurario, Colino comite de Ergile domino Campbel et Lorne cancellario, Archibaldo Augusie comite domino Douglas, Patricio domino Halis magistro hospicii, Roberto domino Lile justiciario, Laurencio domino Oliphant, Andrea domino Gray, Johanne domino Drummond, Magistris Alexandro Inglis archidiacono Sancti Andree computorum rotulatore ac clerico registri et Archibaldo Quhitelaw subdecano Glasguen. secretario.

[22] This very interesting document is recorded in the Register of the Great Seal of Scotland, Lib. XII. No. li.

ACCOUNT OF THE TEMPLARS,

BY

FATHER HAY.

FROM THE ORIGINAL MS. IN THE ADVOCATES' LIBRARY.*

Red Friers or Templars, institut by Pope Gelasius about the year 1117. Their office and vow was to defend the Temple and City of Hierusalem, to entertain Christian strangers, and pilgrims, charitably, and guard them safely through the Holy Land, to view such things as there were to be seen. By the pious liberality of Princes and others well affected, they were in a short time greatly enriched, and for their wealth sore envied and suppressed by Pope Clement the Fifth, rather then for the supposed crimes laid to their charge; anno 1307. All the Kings of Christendome combineing together, caused them, at an instant, to be apprehended within their dominions, confiscated part of their goods, and adjudged the other parts to the Knights or Hospitalers of Saint John of Hierusalem, and those of Jesus Christ in Portugale. In a general council held at Vienna, their substance was disposed of. There was one general Prior that had the governement of this whole order in England and Scotland. Their habit was a white cloak with a red cross, and a sword girt about them. Their successors, the Joannites, or Knights of Malta and Rhodes, had the Hospital of St Germains in Lothian, which house was dissolved in 1494, and the greatest part of its revenues

* This account of the Templars occurs at page 638 of " Ane Account of the
" most renowned Churches, Bishopricks, Monasteries, and other devote Places, from
" the first introduceing of Christianity into Scotland, to the Disturbances occa-
" sion'd in that Nation by the severall Reformations of Religion; with a series of
" the severall Bishops, Abbots, Priors, and other Religious Governours. Written
" by Mr RICHARD AUGUSTINE HAY, Cannon regular of St Genovefs of Paris; Prior
" of St Pierremont. Tome first, 1700." folio, pp. 700.

conferred by King James the Fourth upon the King's College of Aberdeen, then newly founded by Bishop William Elphinston.

Narrat Jacobus de Vitriaco circa annum 1128, cum ex omnibus mundi partibus Hierosolymam visitaturi pergerent Christiani, latrunculos et predatores incautis peregrinis insidiasse, unde quidam devoti milites mundo renunciantes in manu Patriarchæ Hierosol. voto se solemni astrinxerunt, ut a prædictis latronibus peregrinos defenderent, more canonicorum regularium sine proprio in obedientia et castitate militaturi summo Regi, quorum Precipui Hugo de Paganis, et Gaufridus de Sancto Aldemaro. In hoc tam sancto proposito non nisi Novem fuerunt: a principio talibus utebantur vestibus, quales eis in Elemosina largiebantur fideles: novem annis in habitu seculari servierunt: Rex autem et ejus milites ipsis compatientes, una cum Domino Patriarcha de rebus propriis eos sustentabant, quædam beneficia et possessiones eisdem postea pro remedio animarum suarum conferentes; et quoniam nondum proprium habebant domicilium neque certam ecclesiam, Dominus Baldwinus Secundus, Rex, in quadam parte Palatii sui, juxta Templum Domini eisdem ad tempus habitaculum concessit: Abbas autem et Canonici Templi Domini plateam quam habebant juxta Regis Palatium ad opus officinarum eis tradiderunt: inde a mansione juxta Templum patres militiæ Templi appellati sunt; cum autem annis novem sic per-mansissent, anno Domini 1128 de mandato Domini Papæ Honorii, et Domini Stephani Hierosol. Patriarchæ, instituta est eis, regula a Divo Bernardo Clareval: Abbate, 72 distincta Capitulis, et albus habitus, absque cruce assignatus in concilio generali apud Trecas Campaniæ civitatem celebrato, quod Mathæus sanctæ Romanæ ecclesiæ legatus, coegerat, ad prescribendas leges militibus Templariis, quos Gulielmus Newbrigensis appellat mortis Contemptores; De Concilio Trecensi vide notas ad Epist. 39. D. Bernar. Willielmus Tyrius Lib. 12. Belli Sacri Cap. 7. Tandem nono anno concilio in Francia apud Trecas habito 1128, cui interfuerunt Dominus Rhemensis, et Dominus Senonensis, Archiepiscopi, cum suffraganeis suis; Mathæus quoque Albanensis Episcopus, Apostolicæ Sedis Legatus; Abbates quoque Cistertiensis Clarevallensis, et Pontiniacensis cum aliis pluribus instituta est eis regula, et habitus assignatus Albus, viz. de mandato Domini Honorii Papæ et Domini Stephani Hierosolymetani Patriarchæ.

Post modum vero 1146 vel 1148, tempore Eugenii Tertii Papæ
in concilio Rhemis habito, adversus Gilbertum Pictaviensem et Eu-
donem, Hereticos, crux purpurea de panno rubeo, ut inter cæteros
essent notabiliores concessa est militibus Templariis, quam mantellis suis exterius affixerunt, tam equites quam eorum servientes,
ut Carolus Sigonius, Italicarum Rerum author, non contemnendus,
scriptum reliquit, et Jacobus a Vitriaco, lib. 2. cap. 65. Unde
merito arguuntur ab Innocentio Tertio, milites Teutonici, seu
Hospitalis Acconensis, quod in confusionem ordinis alienam vestem
assumerent, et id de cetero fieri jure prohibet, Epist. 725. lib. 1.
Regest. 13. ne ex hoc inter ipsos, et fratres militiæ Templi, quibus in
primordia institutionis ordinis alba pallia concessa fuerant, emula-
tionis et discordiæ materia suscitetur; quod tamen observatum non
fuisse testis est Vitriacus, nam palliis albis deinceps usi sunt Teutonici; eo Solum Adhibito ad Templariorum discrimen, quod
cruces nigras albis chlamidibus assuerunt, utraque ex parte jubente,
Patriarcha Constantinop. vestes albas ex cap. 20. in signum Inno-
centiæ deferebant. Servientibus autem et armigeris vestimentâ
nigra sive burella ex cap. 21. Cruces autem rubeas martyrium de-
signabant, eo quod sanguinem proprium secundum instituta regulæ
pro defensione Terræ Sanctæ effundere sunt professi: Non erat eis
licitum terga fugiendo dare, vel sine mandato a prelio reverti;
Christi adversariis erant formidabiles; vexillum bipartitum ex albo
et nigro, quod nominant "beauciant," prævium habebant, eo quod
Christi Amicis candidi erant et benigni, inimicis nigri et formidabiles. Transgressiones seu negligentias delinquentium fratrum
puniebant, a consortio suo, quosdam irrevocabiliter ejicientes, ablata
cruce rubea, alios usque ad condignam satisfactionem ad terram
absque mappa cibum tenuem sumere injungentes, quibus etiam
canes si forte secum manducarent non liceret amovere; alios etiam
carceribus et vinculis ad tempus vel in perpetuum coercebant. Domino etiam Patriarchæ Hierosolometano a quo professionis princi-
pium et vitæ corporalis subsidium habuerunt, debitam obedientiam
exhibebant; decimas reddebant; milites ex universo mundo, sed et
duces et principes ad eos confluebant, professionis eorum cupientes
esse participes, unde modico tempore adeo multiplicati sunt, quod
in conventu eorum plusquam 300 equites, exceptis servientibus, quorum non erat numerus, omnes albis chlamydibus indutos haberent.

Amplius autem possessionibus, tam citra mare quam ultra dilatati
sunt in immensum, villas, civitates, et oppida, possidentes, ex quibus
certam pecuniæ summam, pro defensione terræ sanctæ, summo eorum
Magistro, cujus sedes principalis erat in Hierusalem mittebant annuatim. Willielmus Tyrius, cap. 7. lib. 12. says, " Possessiones autem
" tam ultra quam citra mare adeo dicuntur immensas habere, ut jam
" non sit in orbe Christiano, provincia, quæ predictis fratribus bono-
" rum suorum portionem non contulerit ; et regiis opulentiis pares
" hodie dicantur habere copias." " Qui cum diu in honesto se conser-
" vassent, proposito, professioni suæ satis prudenter satisfacientes, ne-
" glecta humilitate Domino Patriarchæ Hierosolymitano a quo et
" ordinis institutionem, et prima beneficia susceperant, se subtraxer-
" unt, obedientiam ei quam eorum predecessores eidem exhibuerant
" denegantes : sed et ecclesiis Dei, eis decimas, et primitias subtra-
" hentes, et eorum indebite turbando possessiones, facti sunt valde mo-
" lesti. Quamdiu a prælio abstinebant, nec in castris militiæ et bello
" deputabantur eadem prorsus fuerunt eorum observantiæ, ac canoni-
" corum regularium, jejunia eadem, eædem vigiliæ, idem silentium,
" idem opus manuum quodianum, ac demum mutua quotidianorum
" defectuum proclamatio." Innocen. 3. Epist. 90. Lib. 4. Registri. 16.
Patriarchæ Hierosol. mandat quatenus Magistro et fratribus militiæ
Templi prohibeat ne pro alicujus receptione aliquid exigatur sub pœna
expulsionis, tam in admisso quam in admittente, et regulationis ad
ordinem strictioris observantiæ ; ad concilium generale vocantur ab
Innocentia 3. ab eodem moniti, ut ad defensionem Regis, et Regni
Hierosolymorum intendant. Anno 15. Pontificatus, Epist. 207.
Lib. 3. Regest. 15. Sub Pontificatu Clementis 5. ad annum 1317,
abiere in desuetudinem Pontifex namque ut detestandi facti in-
famiam deleret. Diplomate ad id facto Sodalitium extinxit, et de-
levit. Successore partim equites Rhodii sive Joanitæ, et Hospitalarii,
partim, milites Jesu Christi, in Lusitania vel potius Livonia. They
followed the rule of St Augustine. They possessed above 9000
houses in Christendome. Calixt the Second exim'd them from the
jurisdiction of Bishops, in the Counsell of Rheims 1119 ; and
Alexander the Third from paying of Tithes. It was not allowed
to any one to meddle with them under pain of excommunication.
Philip the Faire, King of France, extinguished them in his dominions. James de Molay, a Gentleman of Burgundy, great mas-

ter of the Templars, was burnt alive at Paris 1313, and several others were execut in other Provinces. Foulques, Prior of Montfaucon, in the Province of Tholok, and a certain man named Woffe-der of Florence, were convicted of several crimes by the Pope's Commissioners. They were accused to adore some images covered with men's skins, to have sacrificed a man, to have burnt a child begotten upon a nun by a Templar, to have rubbed their images over with the grease of a child : whereupon their goods were confiscat in France, and the most part of them put to death. In Germany their goods were only confiscat, and given to the Knights of St Marie. In England they were treated with more humanity.

Dempster says, " Templarii etiam apud nostrates pietatis gloria " non parum floruerunt, qui ordo militaris sacro bello sub Gotfredo " Bullonio exortus pacandis scilicet itineribus, et sancto templo ab " Infidelibus propugnando extinctus per Clementum quintum, Con- " cilio Viennensi, circa annum M.CCCV dixi sæpe in scriptoribus " Scoticis. Hi fratres rubri a nostratibus dicti quod purpura tan- " tum induerentur, plura monasteria in Scotia, et quidem opulen- " tissima possidebant, sed, ego, non potui eruere, unum tantum ad- " notavi, Torphichen ubi Acta ordinis magna cura scribebantur, sed " nunquam in manus meas venerunt." Clemens quintus, bona Mi- litiæ Templi sustulit et ordini Hospitalis Sancti Johannis Hierosol. applicavit. Innocentius Papa vetat ne quis manus injiciat in fugien- tes ad Domus Templariorum sub pœna excommunicationis. Tem- plarii habebant de dono Regis Scotiæ in Ballia de Ogerston villam de Oggerestone, apud Stiuele, et in Gendelaie, in Lindesaia prædia multa, de dono Regis David in Scotia terram de Torphichen, de Fergusio Gallovidiano, Gallwythe. Lib. MS. de Cupro says, " Sanc- " tus David de preclara militia Templi Hierosol. optimos fratres se- " cum retinens eos diebus et noctibus morum suorum fecit esse Cus- " todes." Anno 1118 Hugo de Paganis, Godefridus de Sancto Auda- maro, &c. in manus Patriarchæ Hierosolymorum more canonicorum Regul. vivere sunt professi. Baldwinus Rex in palatio suo juxta Templum domicilium constituit. Matheus Paris primum onus quod eis erat injunctum in remissionem peccatorum fuit quod vias per quas venirent peregrini, custodirent a latronibus, et prædonibus, An. 1307, regni Edwardi secundi, primo die Mercurii proxima, post festum Epiphaniæ; quarto scilicet anno, Papæ Clementis, capti sunt

omnes fratres de Militia Templi, per mandatum Regis, et incarcer-
ati universaliter in Anglia et Francia, et in tota Christianitate,
propter enormitatem professionis suæ et alia superstitiosa, super quibus convicti. In concilio London: omnia eorum bona fuerunt in
manu regis saisita. Anno 1309, factus est processus in Anglia adversus Templarios per Robertum Cantuar: et Radulphum London:
Episcopos in Capitulo monasterii Sanctæ Trinitatis Londoniis de
mandato Domini Clementis Papæ, die Lunæ, solemni examinatione,
articulorum per æmulos objectorum habita, cum nihil inventum
esset quod de jure statum illorum videretur annullare, Clemensque
Papa die Lunæ, 8. Aprilis 1312, in concilio Viennæ habito dammas-
set et inhibuisset, ne quis ordinem ingrediretur de cætero aut habi-
tum illius deferret, sub pœna excommunicationis majoris. Edwardus
Secundus Rex Angliæ sibi metuens juxta ordinationem Clementis
Papæ, Alberto de Nigro Castro, magno Præceptori Hospitalis
Sancti Johannis in Hierusalem, et Leonardo de Tiberiis, Priori
Venetiarum, procuratori generali, Hospitalis predicti, domos et loca
Templariorum assignavit, salvo jure suo. In Parliamento apud
Westmonasterium Anno Regni 17 quod Edwardus Tertius filius
confirmavit, Johannes (Papa) 22. audiens quod nonnulli comites ba-
rones, et personæ ecclesiasticæ in Anglia, manus rapaces extendentes
ad bona Templariorum, post concilium Viennense occupaverant,
Bulla Avignionæ data 15. Kalendas Februarii, anno quarto Pontificatus restituere coegit Hospitulariis. Idem Johannes, Papa,
audiens quod quidam Templarii post sublationem, ordinis vestes
induerent seculares, et matrimonia contraherent, quamvis a concilio Viennensi, non fuissent absoluti a voto religionis, Episcopis
Angliæ scrivit, ut eos moneant quatenus infra tres menses ammoni-
tionis ad aliquam de religionibus approbatis transeant et prelati
monasteriorum quatenus laicos in laicos, et clericos in clericos, tantum recipiant, quod si id facere prelati recusaverint ut saltem in
domibus suis recipiant, compellant tanquam penitentes, stipendiis ad
eorum sustentationem, de domibus Templi assignatis, ita tamen ut
non sint ultra duos in eadem domo. Hujus scripti authoritate, Ro-
gerus Stowe miles Templi transiit ad canonicos regulares Sanctæ
Trinitatis London: erat is presbyter. Multi ad Hospitularios Sancti
Johannis Hierosol. abierunt. (Anno) 1319 Willielmus de Grenefeld
Archiepiscopus Eboracensis pietate motus, super statu Templariorum

suæ diocesis omni auxilio destitutorum eos in diversa monasteria instituit, eisque perpetuo vitæ necessaria ministrari præcepit. Anno 1434 Johannes Stillingfleet librum compilavit de nominibus fundatorum Hospitalis Sancti Johannis in Hierusalem, et Militiæ Templi infra Angliam. Vide tomum secundum, Monast. Angl. Johannes Rex Angliæ, dedit fratribus Templi Hierus. Insulam de Lundeia quæ sita est in Mari, in ore Sabrini fluminis, inter Ginbeth et Bardestapulam. I find one Fulco de Lisuris mentioned in ane inquisitione of the Temple lands of Lindeseie in England. I find Magister et Fratres Templi de Blentodoch vel Blantedroch et Balentradroch mentioned in the Chartular of Newbotle. The principal house of the Templars in Scotland was the Temple near to Southesk in Lothian, possessed at present by James Murray, in whose hands I have seen a manuscript containing all the feu duties belonging to the Templars in Scotland. I heard of him, that, whilst his father was alive, he had found in the garden the foundations of a vast building, and the root of several big pillars of stone, which gave him occasion to believe that they were the foundations of the church.

ACCOUNT OF THE JOANNITES,

OR

KNIGHTS OF ST JOHN.*

Joannites, or Knights of Malta, establish'd by some merchants of the city of Melphe in the kingdome of Naples, who trafick'd in the East, they obtained from the Calife of Egypt, the freedome to build a church att Hierusalem, and a house for those that would come in pilgrimage to the Holy Land. They paid yearly for that effect a tribute. Afterwards they built a church dedicat to our Lady, and ane other to Marie Magdalene, the one for men, the other for women, who were received with all kind of demonstrations of charity. This way of living engaged Gerard, born in the city of Martiques

* From the preceding work, p. 460.

in France, to build a church in honour of Saint John, with ane hospital, in 1099. His reputation gave way to the Kings of Hierusalem, to establish those who had care of the sick and the pilgrims. They were called Hospitaliers. Their habit was black with a cross patè, having eight points, in memory of the eight Beatituds. They made the three ordinary vows of religion, with a fourth, whereby they obliged themselves to receive and defend the pilgrims. The foundation is in 1104. Under Baudwin the first, they went alongst with the pilgrims; and for hindering the incursions of the Saracens, they were obliged to make use of offensive arms. This employment drew several persons of quality amongst them, whereby they became Knights. And to this day they declare war to the enemies of our faith. Gerard formed their statuts, and his successor put them in a better form in 1118. His body was carried in 1534 from Rhodes to Mavesque in Provence, where his bones are visited with great devotion, and many miracles are alleged to be wrought there. After the taking of Hierusalem, the Knights retired to Margate: Afterwards to Acre, which place they held out against the Turke in 1290. They followed John of Luzignan, who gave them in his kingdom of Cyprus, Limisson, where they abode till 1310; in which year they were transported to Rhodes, and held it out the year following against an army of Saracens, with the help of ane Earl of Savoy, whose successors have this device, F. E. R. T. which signifies, Fortitudo ejus Rhodum tenuit; from whence they were stiled Knights of Rhodes. Mahomet the Second laid siege to this isle without success in 1480, and Solomon took it in 1522. Adrian the Sixth gave to Philip de Villiers L'Isle Adam, great maistre, and to his Knights, the city of Viterbe for retreat. Six years after, viz. 1530, they were placed in Malta by Charles the Fifth, who granted them that Isle to put Sicilly out of danger. The Knights accepted, with the agreement of all the Christian Princes in whose dominions the order had any lands. In 1566 Solyman besieged Malta; the siege lasted four months, after which the Turks retired, having lost 15,000 soldiers and 8000 mariners. Since, the Isle is pretty well fortified. The order was at that time composed of eight languages or nations. Since the schisme in England, there are only seven. The first is that of Provence, the head whereof is great commendator of the order. The second is that of Auvergne, the head whereof is Marshall of the order. The third is that of France, the head whereof is great Hospitalier. The fourth is that of Italy, and the head is Admiral. The fifth is that of Arrogan, and the chief thereof is great Conservator. The sixth is that of Germany, and the chief thereof is great Bailif. The seventh is that of Castile, and the chief great Chancellor. England was of old the sixth, and the chief was great Turcopelier, or colonel of cavalry. The Knights must make proof of their birth, and justifie their nobility for four races, both on the father's side and mother's. They must be of 20 years of age, and be born in lawful marriage. The bastards of Kings and Princes are excepted. The only Knights, called Le Grands Croix, can be created Great Master. Les Chevaliers, servants are commonly of ane honest family. Their courage is seen in the constant wars they have with the Turk. They make all the vows, and live without marrying. Their command in Scotland were at Torphiphen and Currey. The first was named Lord Saint John from the Hospitale.

Raymundus de Podio Puy secundus Magister Hopitalis Sancti Johannis mansiones edificavit fratribus et regulam prescripsit quam amiserant in captione Civitatis Anconensis: hanc Eugenius Papa confirmavit; Bonifacius item, 8 Laterani 7 Idus Aprilis, Anno 6 Pontificatus sui. Non debebant fratres petere amplius quam panem aquam, et vestitum. Clerici ad altare albis vestibus utebantur; fratres bis in die comedebant. Quarta feria et Sabbatho a septuagesima a Pascha carnes non comedebant. Fornicator publicus die Dominica in villa ubi facinus admisit, publice a magistro vel aliis corrigiis, vel virgis flagellabatur, et post e societate expellebatur. Si poeniteat, post annum in loco extraneo, exactum recipiebatur. Siquis cum altero fratre, altercabatur, septem diebus in terra comedebat sine mensa et manu tergio. In cappis et mantellis crucem omnes deferebant. Largitione Principum et eleemosinis piorum crevit ordo iste, et sumptus magnos apposuit ut absolveretur ab obedientia Patriarchæ Hierosol. et Episcoporum quibus multas molestias inferebant, quo facto decimas ab ecclesiis vicinis tollebant, quas gravabant: per dona curiam Romanam corrumpebant: excommunicatos sepeliebant in cemeteriis suis, et ad Missas admittebant, et si quæ civitas esset excommunicata, in qua degerent, faciebant Hospitalarii fortius pulsare campanas: in parochiis suis Presbyteros quos volebant inconsultis Episcopis ponebant. Jordanus Briset fundavit Hospitale sancti Joannis Hyerosolimitani in suburbio Londinensi anno 1100 Henrici primi regno anno 1185, sexto idus Martii, ecclesia dicti Hospit. dedicata est ab Eracleo Patriarcha Hierosolimitano.*

* Hay's MS. Collections are in the Advocates' Library, and a very full account of them drawn up by the late Mr George Paton of the Custom-House, will be found in Gough's British Topography, Vol. II. p. 611, 612, 737 to 739.—In a letter, dated 6th Aug. 1779, from the latter to the former, there occurs the following notices relative to him. The Faculty of Advocates " bought Mr Richard " Hay's MSS. much about the time of his decease; but it would seem no minute of " this transaction seems to have been entered in their register, which has hitherto " prevented my furnishing you with the date of his death, yet have not desisted " my search, so expect to obtain it, though not so early as may answer your purpose. " Lord Auchinleck was intimate with him; his Lordship being much afflicted with " various complaints that have put many articles of his earlier days out of memory, " this particular incident he cannot so truly recollect; (I) do not despair of get-" ting the intelligence." Notwithstanding the extreme industry of both these gentlemen, it seems to have escaped their notice that in 1720 Father Hay issued " Proposals for printing the Chronicle of John Fordun, with the additions and con-" tinuations of Walter Bowmaker, Abbot of Inch-Colm," &c. The proposed title was as follows: " Scoti-chronicon sive Joannis Forduni, de rebus apud Scotos " gestis, a primo Gentis Conditore, ad exitum Davidis Primi, Regis, Libri Octo. " Quibus accedunt, Walteri Monasterii D. Columbæ in Æmona insula, Abbatis, " Historiarum Libri 32. Ab anno Christianæ salutis 1153, quo anno David Rex, " gravi Morbo absumptus est Kaerleoli ad Jacobi primi Regis Interitum. Ex " M. S. Codice B. M. de Cupro, Cisterciensis Instituti, nunc primum editi, Opera " Richardi Hayi Edinburgeni. Cum indice Rerum et Verborum Alphabetico ad " Calcem Notarum." • This projected work, which was to cost " ten shillings ster-" ling at subscribing, and as much at the delivery of the printed copy," seems to have met with no encouragement, and was given up. It is proper to mention, that from the extreme inaccuracy of the quotation from Dempster, the Editor struck out Father Hay's incorrect version, and has restored the passage as it occurs in the " Apparatus ad Historiam Scoticam," " Bononiæ," 1622, 4to, p. 79.

the lands within these bailiaries, at least many more than are hitherto discovered, are Temple Lands, and as such are comprehended under the petitioner's right of regality constituted as said is over the whole Temple Lands within these bailiaries.

This jurisdiction standing now abolished by the late act of Parliament, and the petitioner being thereby entitled to obtain a just satisfaction or recompence for the same, upon a claim to be entered before your Lordships, in the form and manner by the aforesaid statute directed, he now claims £2000 Sterling as an equitable and just satisfaction for that office and jurisdiction, which the law compels him to part with.

> May it therefore please your Lordships to find your petitioner entitled to the foresaid heritable office of regality, of all and whole the Temple Lands and tenements situated within the bailiaries of Kylestewart and Kingskyle, and to value and appretiate the same to the above-mentioned sum of £2000 Sterling, and to certify such your opinion to his Majesty in his Privy Council.

> According to justice, &c.

> ALEX. LOCKHART.

January 15. 1748.
Objections and Defences for His MAJESTY'S ADVOCATE in behalf of the Crown, against the Claim of Sir JOHN CUNNINGHAM of Caprington, Bart.

The petitioner claims the office or privilege of regality over all the Temple Lands within the regality of Kylestewart and Kingskyle, and suggests as the value £2000.

The claimant has produced a progress beyond forty years to the Temple Lands lying within the bailliaries of Kylestewart, of old part of the Lordship of Torphichen, which writs bear a clause " cum " privilegio liberæ regalitatis infra integras dictas terras Templarias;"

and these lands are erected into a free tenandry called Temple; and for this privilege of regality the claimant demands £2000.

The respondent, without entering into the question how far the Lordship of Torphichen was properly erected into a regality, shall content himself with observing, that the lands in this claim mentioned, having been sold off, and charters taken from the crown of them, were thereby dismembered from the regality, if ever such was erected; and therefore, unless they had been of new erected into a separate regality, no jurisdiction of regality was competent, and no such thing appears to have been done; the erection being into a tenandry, not into a regality; and the respondent is informed, that no exercise of this jurisdiction can be instructed; so that, in conformity to the decision in the case of the Earl of Morton, the claimant's title falls to be rejected.

ALEX. BOSWELL.*

ABSTRACT of various Claims of Heritable Jurisdiction over detached parts of the Regality of Torphichen.†

1. John Campbell of Calder claimed (Nov. 9. 1747) £500 sterling as the value of the heritable bailliary of the Temple Lands of Ardarsier in the shire of Inverness. He also claimed the value of the heritable Sheriffship of Nairn, and the heritable Constabulary of

* The claim was rejected.

† As all these claims, from their reference to the grant by Queen Mary, are pretty much the same, and as they throw no additional light on the history of the Templars, it was judged inexpedient to do any thing than give a brief abstract of them. They will be found in the Collection of Jurisdiction Papers in the Advocates' Library.

the Castle of Nairn. The former was dismissed, but the latter was admitted.*

2. David Viscount of Stormont claimed (Nov. 9. 1747) £2000 as the value of the Lordship of the regality of the Temple Lands and Temple Tenements within the shire of Perth. His claim was dismissed.†

3. John Earl of Stair claimed, (Nov. 9. 1747,) *inter alia*, £100, as the value of the privilege of regality of the Temple Lands of Philipston, and £100, of the Lands of Breastmiln,‡ both portions of the regality of Torphichen in Galloway. Claim dismissed.

4. Hon. Mr William Gordon of Fyvie (Nov. 10. 1747) claimed the value of the lordship, regality, and barony, of Fyvie, " formerly called Fermertine," or " Foremarten," a part of the patrimony of Alexander Earl of Dunfermline, who acquired right to "certain Tem-

---

* The Lord Advocate's defence is valuable, from the reference it makes to the old titles of the Calder family. " The claimant's titles to the offices of Sheriff " of Nairn, and Constable of the Castle of Nairn, are old beyond exception ; there " being produced a seasine, in favour of Donald thane of Calder, one of the claim- " ant's ancestors, proceeding on a precept granted by Robert Duke of Albany, in " the year 1405, for infefting the said Donald as heir, served and retoured to An- " drew his father, in the heritable offices of Sheriff of Nairne, and Constable of the " Castle of Nairn ; and the claimant has produced writs, proving his descent from " the aforesaid Donald thane of Calder, by Murellia Calder, heiress of Calder, who " was married to John Campbell, knight, son of the family of Argyle in the 1511, " and a connected later progress to himself; so that the grant, in favour of the " claimant's predecessor, of these offices being long prior to the time mentioned in " the act of James II. was valid and unexceptionable, and the exercise of the office " of Sheriff immemorially is notorious." His Lordship objected, however, to the amount of the sum demanded, viz. £3000 for the Sheriffship, and £500 for the office of Constable. This last was dismissed, but £2000 was allowed for the former.

† His Lordship founded on a grant from Lord Torphichen, and set up a title to the whole Temple Lands in Perthshire, although he had right only to a portion of them ; his ancestor having, in order to prevent a reduction at the instance of Lord Binning, restricted his interest to certain Temple Lands in the town of Perth and village of Scoon, and a few others specially named and described. The bond of re-striction is recorded in the books of Council and Session, and is dated March 7. 1615.

‡ The lands of Breastmiln are said to have been acquired from one James Dun-das, who sold them in 1723 to the then Earl of Stair.

" ple Lands, part of the regality of Torphichen, lying locally within
" the Lordship of Fyvie ; and these Temple Lands were given off
" with the right and privilege of regality, and office of bailliary."
Charles Earl of Dunfermline was served heir in special to Earl
Alexander his father in 1633 *inter alia*, in the lordship, which
passed by progress to William Earl of Aberdeen, who in his marriage contract with Lady Anne Gordon, daughter of Alexander
Duke of Gordon, settled the lordship of Fyvie upon the claimant.
His claim (for £1000) was dismissed.

5. William Henry, Marquis of Lothian (Nov. 10. 1747) claimed
£1000 as the value of his jurisdiction over the Temple Lands of
Oxnam, Temple Lands of Ormiston, and other Temple Lands in
the county of Roxburgh, part of the old Lordship of Torphichen.
He gave no account of the way in which the superiority of these
lands came into his family, but founded upon a prescriptive title,
producing a connected progress from the year 1700. His claim
was dismissed.

6. Mr William Wallace, Advocate, claimed £500 for the office
of bailliary and jurisdiction of regality over the Temple Lands in
the bailliary of Cunninghame. The original claim is not preserved
by Elchies, but, from the defences for the Lord Advocate, it would
seem that his title was merely an adjudication obtained upon the
10th November 1767, which was not extracted when the claim was
entered. Lord Elchies has jotted down, " dismissed."

7. It would appear from a claim given in by John Gillon of Wallhouse (Nov. 10. 1747) that the lands of Wallhouse, South and
North Hilderstouns, Torphichen Mill, and other lands, were originally held under the Lordship of St John, as he mentions that they
formed part of the Regality of Torphichen, and that he had acquired
the superiority thereof, and right of regality, by purchase from
James Lord Torphichen. Mr Gillon states, he had procured a
crown charter of resignation under the great seal upon the 22d,
upon which infeftment followed the 29th June 1733. He claimed
£300 as the value, but his claim was dismissed.

LETTERS of Replegiation by JAMES Lord TORPHICHEN, to Mr ROBERT LINTON, Advocate.

3d February 1593.

BE it kend till all men be thir present letters, We James Sandelandis of Calder lord of Torphechin and Regalitie thairof, with expres consent and assent of our curatouris undersubscrivand for thair enteresse statutes and ordaines our louit Mr Robert Lintoun* aduocat coniunctlie and seuerallie our verray lauful vndowtit and Irreuocable baillies of our Regalitie foirsaid in that pairt to the effect vnderwrittin allanerlie, Geuand, grantand, and committand, to our saids baillies, coniunctlie and seuerallie, our verie full, free, plane power, speciall mandement, expres bidding, and charge, for ws, and in our name, all and sindrie our men, tennentis, seruandis, inhabitantis, and indwellaris, within oure pairt of our said Regalitie of Torphechen, being or that sall happin to be callit, attechit, arreistit, accusit, or dilatit, befoir our soueraine lords Justice, and his deputtis, or vthir Juge, or Judges spiritual, or temporal, within this realme, for quhatsumevir actioun, or cause criminall or civil, To the privilege and freedome of our said Regalitie and courtis thairof, To be haldin at Torphechin before our baillie of our said regalitie, To Reduce, repledge, burrow, and agane bring cawtioun of collerauth† for iustice to be ministrat, to pairteis complenand, within terme of law, To geue and find courtis thairvpoun neidfull, To assigne ane Limit, Protestationes to mak, and generallie all vthir and sindrie

---

* Linton held a commission of bailliarie from Lord Torphichen and his curators, dated 6th and 8th of August, 1589.

† See Skene (*De Verborum Significatione*), who calls the word "Culrach." It means a pledge that the individual who re-pledges shall do justice within a year and day, in his own court, to the party complaining, upon the person re-pledged.

thingis to do, vs, have, and exerce, that in the premisses is necessar to be doin, or that we micht do ourselffis being personallie present, quhilk we sall hald ferme and stable be thir presents, In Witness heirof to thir present letters (of) replegiacioun subscryvit be ws and our saids curators for thair entress, In taking of thair consent to the premisses, our seill is affixt, At Edinburgh, the thrid day of February, 1593 zeiris, befoir thir witnesses, harie stewart of Craigyhall, Mr John broun, Mr James Spottiswood, our seruands, Mr John Spottiswood, parsoun of Calder, and vtheris diverse.*

* From a copy preserved in the Chartulary of Torphichen. The following entry relative to Mr Robert Linton occurs previously in the volume, (p. 40.) " A gift to " Mr Robert lintoun for his pensioun of ten punds vj & viij^d of the few maillis and " landis of Gatua (Galtua in Galloway) for seruice done and to be done be him to " the Lord Torphechin as baillie of the Regalitie, and as pursuer in all actiones be- " foir the Lords of Counsall, Sheriff and Commissars of Edinburgh and otheris in- " feriour Judges, of the dait the sext of May 1586." A very small gratification, for the trouble Mr Linton must have had. The present letters of replegiation were made necessary by the death of the first Lord Torphichen, when the old ones fell by the demise of the granter.

CLAIM for James Lord Torphichen, to the Regality of the Barony of Torphichen.

November 10, 1747.

Unto the Right Honourable the Lords of Council and Session, the Petition and Claim of James Lord Torphichen;

Sheweth,

That Sir James Sandilands, Lord St John, Preceptor of Torphichen, having made resignation of all the Temple Lands of Scotland into the hands of Queen Mary, her Majesty, with consent of the three Estates of Parliament, did, by her charter dated the 24th of January 1563, for payment of 10,000 crowns, and of a yearly duty of 500 merks, feu out again to the said James Lord St John, his heirs, and assignees, the Barony of Torphichen, and certain other lands therein mentioned, " cum omnibus privilegiis, immuni-
" tatibus, præeminentiis, dignitatibus, officiis, regalitatibus, et cum li-
" bera capella et cancellaria infra omnes bondas dictarum terra-
" rum, per dict. Jacobum et suos prædecessores tanquam præceptores
" de Torphichen aliquo tempore ante datam præsentium possessa-
" rum.

" Ac eximimus ipsius tenentes et dictarum terrarum suarum oc-
" cupatores, ab omni comparentia coram quocunque judice aut ju-
" dicibus, criminalibus aut civilibus, spiritualibus seu temporalibus
" nisi coram præfati Jacobi propriis balivis prædict. terrarum, per ip-
" sum, heredes suos, et assignatos, deputatis seu deputandis, aut coram
" Dominis nostræ Sessionis, tantum submittendo illos ipsorum juris-
" dictione solum in hac parte : et exonerando similiter omnes alios
" judices et juris ministros, ab omni processione contra ipsos aut ip-
" sorum aliquem et ab illorum officiis in hac parte, in perpetuum."

And upon this charter, infeftment followed the 4th of May 1564.

That your petitioner, as nearest heir to the said James Lord St

John, is lawfully possessed of the Lordship and Barony of Torphichen, and certain other lands mentioned in the said charter, and is legally entitled to the jurisdiction of regality granted by the above charter; which he and his predecessors have immemorially possessed and exerced in as ample a manner as any other Lord of Regality.

That your petitioner has produced such of his titles as are in his hands; and must pray for a diligence from your Lordships to recover the writs that are in the hands of others relative thereto.

That, in pursuance of the late statute, enacted in the 20th year of his present Majesty, entitled an act for taking away and abolishing the heritable jurisdictions in that part of Great Britain called Scotland, and for making satisfaction to the proprietors thereof, &c. the petitioner does hereby enter his claim for the value or price of the said regality, and prays that your Lordships may find, that he is lawfully possessed of and justly entitled thereto; and that you will give your opinion concerning the value thereof, as by the statute is directed.

And as your Lordships have, by your ordinance of the 4th instant, directed that all claims should express the sum claimed as the value of the jurisdiction, your petitioner does, in obedience thereto, suggest the sum of £2000 sterling as the value of the said regality; at the same time submitting the whole entirely to your Lordships, to be determined according to such rules as shall appear to be just and equitable, when this, and other cases of the like nature, are taken under your consideration.

May it therefore please your Lordships to grant diligence, at your petitioner's instance, against havers, for recovering any of the titles of the above jurisdiction of regality, or any other writs necessary to astruct (instruct) or support the validity thereof, or to clear the nature, extent, or limits of the same; and to find that your petitioner is lawfully possessed of, and justly entitled to the said jurisdiction, and to consider and declare your opinions touching the value and price thereof; and to cause such opinion to be entered in a roll or book, and make certificate thereof to his Majesty in his Privy Council, according to the form of the statute above mentioned.

According to Justice, &c.

JAMES FERGUSON.

11*th January* 1748.

DEFENCES or Objections for his MAJESTY's ADVOCATE, in behalf of the Crown, against the Claims of JAMES Lord TORPHICHEN.

His Lordship claims, as Lord of the regality of Torphichen, £2000.

The respondent must observe upon his Lordship's title, 1st, That the charter by Queen Mary in 1563, referred to by his Lordship, does not seem to give a right of regality; for by it all that is granted is the Barony of Torphichen and others therein mentioned, lying within the Sheriffdoms of Edinburgh, Peebles, and five other different counties therein mentioned, " Nec non omnes annuos reditus, " terras templarias, decimas, loca, possessiones, et alias terras quas- " cunque, tam non nominátas, quam nominatas, infra regnum Scotiæ " existen. cum omnibus privilegiis, immunitatibus, præeminentiis, " dignitatibus, officiis, regalitatibus, cum libera capella et cancellaria " infra bondas quarumcunque terrarum, per dictum Dominum Ja- " cobum Sandilands, aut suos prædecessores, tanquam præceptores " de Torphichen, aliquo tempore ante datam presentium possess."

This is the only grant of jurisdiction which his Lordship has produced ; and as it does not give right to any special jurisdiction, but refers to the powers which were competent to the Preceptors of Torphichen, it will be incumbent upon his Lordship to shew, that the Preceptors of Torphichen had a right of regality of the barony of Torphichen, or any of the lands over which his Lordship now claims that jurisdiction, otherwise the grant being altogether relative, cannot be available.

Neither will the clause in the foresaid grant 1563, exeeming the inhabitants of the said Barony from compearance before any court civil or criminal, spiritual or temporal, except the Lord St John's, or the Lord Torphichen's proper baillie, and the Lords of Session, in the respondent's apprehension, be sufficient to create a jurisdiction, either civil, criminal, or spiritual; for jurisdiction is not to be granted by implication,

The respondent, 2dly, objects to his Lordship's title, that the lands over which the regality is claimed, were lands which of old belonged to a religious order, viz. the Knights of St John of the

Hospital of Jerusalem, who got them upon the suppression of the Knights Templars, and was governed by a preceptor, who was called Lord of St John; and though by the act of annexation 1587, the Lordship of Torphichen be declared not to fall under the annexation, but to remain with the person to whom it was granted; yet, by the 13th act, Parl. 1st, Charles I. entituled, Anent Regalities of Erections, "his Majesty, with consent of the Estates of Parliament, " casses, annuls, retreats, and rescinds, all writs and titles made and " granted by his Majesty, or his Majesty's umquhile father, or by " umquhile Queen Mary his grandmother, of the right and privilege " of regality pertaining to whatsoever Abbot, Prior, Prioress, Pre- " ceptor, or other beneficed person whatsoever, at any time preced- " ing the date hereof; and declares the right and title of all and " whatsoever regalities within the kingdom, which pertained to " whatsoever benefice particularly or generally above specified, at " any time preceding the general annexation of kirk lands, without " respect to any exception mentioned in the said act of annexation " to pertain to his Majesty in all time coming."

As therefore, by the act just now mentioned, any regality powers which may be supposed to have been granted by the charter 1563 were annulled, the same could not again be revived, on account of sundry statutes, and particularly the act 53. Parl. 1. Sess. 1. Charles II. whereby all grants of new regalities over kirk lands are declared to be null, and that by way of exception or reply. And besides, in this case, it does not appear that any new grant after 1633 was made; for the latest right produced by his Lordship is in the 1622; and the respondent cannot, from his information, admit that the claimant or his predecessors, have been in use to hold regality courts, and exerce regality powers.

With respect to the value claimed by his Lordship, upon the supposal of a proper title, the respondent apprehends the same to be excessive; in regard it appears from sundry claims now entered, that many of the lands over which this jurisdiction, whatever it was, originally extended, are now alienated, or dismembered, and ex- eemed from it; and how much remains still with his Lordship, is not set forth in the claim, nor the extent or valuation thereof, or the possession instructed.

ALEX. BOSWELL.

CONDESCENDENCE for the Lord TORPHICHEN, and Inventory of the Writs produced relative thereto, for instructing his Possession of the Regality claimed.

In obedience to an order of Court, the claimant herewith produces an inventory and condescendence of what writs are presently in his hands, for instructing his possession of the regality of Torphichen. And though he apprehends the production he now makes is sufficient to satisfy the Court of his having been past the years of prescription in the exercise of that jurisdiction, yet he would have been able to have given more full evidence thereof, had it not been, that Hugh Anderson, who was clerk to the said regality in the year 1729, as appears by his commission produced, and who as such, fell to be possessed of the court books, and papers belonging thereto, went off the country abruptly several years ago, without delivering up these books and papers, and is now settled in America. Though the claimant has of late made diligent search, in order to recover those books and papers, he has only been able to pick up here and there the papers he now produces. But for books, he can recover none ; though he is able to instruct, by parole evidence, that books were kept, and that past memory of man he has, by his baillies, been in the constant and regular course of holding regality courts. Having premised this, the claimant shall proceed to state the documents produced, which are as follows :—

1mo, Commission by the claimant to Patrick Stone, writer in Linlithgow, to be clerk to the said regality, dated the 19th August 1700, and marked on the back to have been recorded in the said court books upon the 20th of said month.

2do, Commission by ditto to Hugh Anderson, writer in Edinburgh, to be clerk to said regality, dated 24th November 1729.

3tio, Commission by ditto to Mr Walter Sandilands, Advocate, constituting and appointing him bailie of the regality, with a power to name substitutes, dated the 12th November 1733.

4to, Commission by said Mr Walter Sandilands in favours of John Ferrier, Writer in Linlithgow, appointing him one of his substitutes, dated the 16th November 1741.

5to, Thirteen different suit rolls of said regality.

6to, A bundle of decreets and warrants from the year 1702 to the 1746.

Lastly, The claimant produces a paper found in his own charter chest, being part of the progress of some lands the family had afterwards purchased, viz. a precept by John Lord Torphichen for infefting of Sarah, Margaret, and Isabel Lilies, in certain subjects therein mentioned, as heirs to their father, conform to their service before the bailie of his regality, retoured to his own chancery. This precept is dated the 27th July 1635.

The above document, which is by accident in the claimant's hands, proves the exercise of the jurisdiction very early after the 1633; and that it was not then understood that this jurisdiction was abolished by that law, as is now pled on the other side; and the claimant can prove, if the Lords thinks it necessary, by unexceptionable evidence, that there have been regular head courts held in this regality three times a year, for above forty years past; though, by the accident of the clerk's going off the country, the books and suit rolls are amissing. But he hopes, what is already produced, will satisfy the Lords, that the jurisdiction has been duly exercised, so as to entitle the claimant to the recompence allowed by the act of Parliament.

The claimant has further produced his chartulary, by which it appears, that the lands held of him, are in his vassals charters, uniformly designed to lie within the Barony and Regality of Torphichen; and the respective vassals are always taken bound to give suit and presence at the three head courts yearly; and as they are all laid under this obligation by their charters, so their attendance at the regality head courts can be proven as far back as the memory of man goes.*

JAMES FERGUSON.

* Lord Elchies Notes, " Sustain, in respect of more than forty years possession." The sum of £134 : 12 : 6 was allowed. See Acts of Sederunt, p. 425.

CLAIM for Sir JOHN CUNNINGHAM of Caprington, Bart. to the Regality of the Temple Lands, with the Bailliaries of Kylestewart and Kingskyle, united into the Tenendry of Temple.

November 9, 1747.

Unto the Right Honourable the Lords of Council and Session, the Petition of Sir JOHN CUNNINGHAM of Caprington, Baronet;

Humbly sheweth,

That Mary Queen of Scots having received resignation *ad remanentiam* from the last preceptor of Torphichen of all the Temple Lands in Scotland, did erect these into a temporal Lordship in favours of the Lord Torphichen.

That this erection in favours of the Lord Torphichen continues to be the sovereign title for all these lands wherever situated : many are lost, and cannot now be discovered; but wherever discovery is made, which daily happens to be the case, the Vassals in these lands are obliged to acknowledge the Lord Torphichen, or those who stand in his right, as their superiors, take charters from them, and submit to these jurisdictions, which had anciently been established.

King Charles II. by charter under the Great Seal herewith produced, of date December 1. 1682, proceeding upon the resignation of John Earl of Glencairn, granted and disponed to Sir John Cunningham of Lambruchtoun, and the heirs male of his body, &c. the several lands, baronies, offices, and jurisdictions therein contained; and more particularly " omnes et singulas et quascunque terras tem-
" plarias, et tenementa, tam proprietatem, quam tenendriam earun-
" dem, ubicunque eædem jacent. infra integras bondas balliatus de
" Kylestewart, et Kingskyle, quæ pertinere dignoscuntur, seu per-
" tinuisse dignosci poterint dominio seu præceptorio de Torphichen,

" quovis tempore præterito, cum privilegio liberæ regalitatis juxta
" integras dictas terras templarias, et tenementa, cum omnibus suis
" pertinen. jacen. intra omnes limites dict. balliatuum de Kyle-
" stewart, et Kingskyle, cum omnibus et singulis aliis privilegiis, im-
" munitatibus, casualitatibus, &c. dictarum terrarum templariarum,
" et tenementorum ùbicunque jacent. infra dictum balliatum eisdem
" spectan. seu juste spectare valen. et quibus ulli præceptorum seu
" dominorum de Torphichen et St John gavisi sunt quovis tempore
" præterito, aut in antiquis evidentiis, infeofamentis, erectione ejus-
" dem dominii, et preceptorii content. vel quæ sunt content. in infeof-
" amentis acquisit. per quondam Jacobum dominum de Torphichen
" et St John, a nostra quondam charissima proavia Maria Scoto-
" rum Regina beatæ memoriæ. Quæquidem decimæ, terræ tem-
" plariæ aliaque suprascript, &c. uniuntur, eriguntur, creantur, et
" incorporantur, in unam integram et liberam tenendriam nuncupat.
" tenendriam de Temple."

That Sir William Cunningham of Capringtoun, your petitioner's
father, was in the year 1685 served and retoured heir in special to
the foresaid Sir John Cunningham his father; and, by virtue of
the precept of sasine issuing upon the foresaid retour, was duly infeft in the premises, as in like manner appears from the instrument
of sasine herewith produced.

That though your petitioner has not hitherto completed his own
right by infeftment, he possesses the estate of Caprington upon the
title of apparency, as heir to his father, who died last vest and seized therein. What the extent may be of the whole Temple Lands
within these bailiaries of Kylestewart and Kingskyle, is more than
the petitioner can take upon him to affirm; such of them as have
been discovered, have taken charters from, and otherwise acknowledged, your petitioner's predecessors superiority and jurisdiction over
these lands, considerable parcels whereof belonging in property to
the heirs of Provost Samuel Muir, merchant in Ayr, Bailies Neil and
Blair, and Gilbert Doig in Prestick, William Kelso of Danketh,
Alexander Fairly of that Ilk, Captain Alexander Nugent of New-
field, John Cunningham of Munktonhill, George Brown of Knock-
marnock, the heirs of James Rae of Walston, and Farquhar of Gil-
merscroft, ly in the parishes of Ayr, Munkton, Symington, Dun-
donald, Riccarton, Craigie, and Muckland; and as new discoveries
are daily making, there is reason to believe that a great many of

CHARTA Magistri Hospitalis S. Jọ. Hierios. Digneto Scott.*

FRATER Johannes de Lascico Dei Gratia Sacræ Domus hospitalis S. Hierosol. Magister Humilis, Pauperumque ibidem Christi Custos, Discreto viro fideli, Dilecto nostro Digneto Le Scott, Salutem in Domino Sempiternam. Propter multiplicia virtutum tuarum merita et propter laudabilia atque diuturna obsequia per te nobis, ac relligione nostræ, citra et ultra mare, fideliter et sollicitè præstita, rationabiliter moti sũmus ut tibi reddamur ad gratias liberales, quo in futurum commode vivere possis, et alii simili exemplo ad serviendum nobis et dictæ relligioni ferventius animentur: cum itaque his super dudum super domo sive familia nostra de Torphequyn in Scotia situat. Scuta auri decem annis singulis donec vixeris in humanis percipienda tibi concessimus; et [cum] de dictis decem scutis commode vivere non possis, præmissorum obsequiorum per te præstitorum, et quæ impendere quotidie non desistis, intuitu et contemplatione moti, scuta alia decem de specialis doni S. Gra. super dicta Præceptoria nostra, vid. super pensione annua vobis ex eadem debita sive debenda, donec vitam duxeris in humanis per te annis singulis vel alios tuo nomine percipienda de bono auro, et justi ponderis, Tenore præsentium tibi assignamus; ita quod a primo festo S. Johannis futuri, vita ut premittitur durante tua recipere possis Scuta viginti, hoc est decem tibi prius largita, et alia decem quæ tibi de præsenti largimur, a Preceptore presenti, sive futuro mandari eisdem preceptoribus tam moderno quam futuro in eadem Domo constituend. aut presidend. in eadem, quatenus de summa annuæ pensionis vobis debeter ex domo nostra prædicta, Scuta 20 tibi vel tuis procuratoribus sub virtute Sanctæ

* From Father Hay's MS. Collections, Advocates' Library.

A

obedientiæ annuatim solvere curent: Promittentes bona fide eandem summam nomine dictæ pensionis infalibiliter defalcare, et pro soluta realiter et cum effectu perceptar. universis et singulis Domus nostræ prædictæ fratribus quacunque authoritate, dignitate officiove fungentur, præsentibus et futuris, sub eadem Sanctæ obedientiæ virtute districte injungimus, ac præcipiendo mandamus, ne contra nostram præsentem assignationem et gratiam tibi per nos factam, verbo vel opere, publice vel occulte, per se vel per alios impositas personas, temere venire præsumant, quinimo eandem juxta sui tenorem et continentiam studeant inviolabiliter observare. In cujus rei testimonium Bulla nostra Magistralis plumbea præsentibus est appensa. Datum Rhod. in nostro conventu die 12 Mensis Junii Anno ab incarnatione Domini 1442.

Hujus Litteræ captum fuit instrumentum et petitum transumptum a Patricio de Cockburn præposito, Ballivis Jacobo Batbuy et sociis, anno Do. 1448.*

* This grant is printed, without variation, from the copy in Father Hay's Collection. There appear to be some inaccuracies, which my inability to procure the original, rendered it impossible to correct.

COMMISSION

By James, the first Lord Torphichen, to Robert Lyndsay of Dunrod,

20th July, 1570.

Be it kend till all men be thir present letters, Me James Lord of Torphichan, Forsamekle as I haue alreddie made and constitute, my weilbelouit Robert Lyndsay of Dunrod, my Justice generale, and baillie principale and speciale, of all and sindrie my landis and lordschip of Torphichan, Listoun, Ballintrodo, Tankartoun, Denny, Mariecultar, Stanehop, and Galtoway, with all and sindrie vthiris my tempill landis, annexis and connexis, thairof quhatsumevir, liand within quhatsumevir sherefdome of this realme, for the space of nynetene zeiris; with power to hald Justice airis, Justice courtis, and Baillie courtis, and to vse and exerceis all vthir thingis belanging to the offices of iusticiare, and baillerie; as at mair lenth is conteint in the power grantit thairvpoun: And becaus I, vndirstanding myself to be vnhable in persone, to pas and trawaill at oistis, raidis, airmeis, or conventionis, and to sustene the surfite chairgis thairof, in cawld, trawaill, walking, and vthiris chairgis requisit thairto, without extreme dainger and parrell of my life, throw the inhabilitie of my persone, in that behalf; Thairfor, to have gevin, and grantit, lykeas I, be the tennor heirof, gifis, and grantis, my full plane power, to the said Robert Lyndsay, my baillie foirsaid, during all the tyme of his office thairof, to convene, gadder, raiss, and vplift, all and sindrie my tennenttis, frehaldaris, wassellis, and vthiris inhabitantis (of) my saidis landis, astrictit for seruice, alsueill to our souerane Lordis weiris, as my seruice, at all tymes necessare and requisite for the same, to pas with him, await vpoun his seruice, baith to our souerane Lord, and my awin proper seruice, in all and quhatsumevir leissum actionis and caussis, as the said baillie sall require thame;

and vndir sic paines, as thai mycht incurr, in caice thai wer chairgit
be my self thairto ; and to that effect, with power to my said baillie,
to hald wappinschawing, tak in cumpanie with him the maist able
men, taxt and stent the remanent, for the furthbringing and susstein-
ing thame, as vse and consuetude is, obseruit within this realme in sic
caissis; and to uptak the (haill) panis (and) vnlawis, of the personis dis-
sobeyand, and to apply the same to his awin vse, for his lauboris, and
diligence : And gif neid be, to poind and distreinzie thairfore, or to
dispone to vthiris thairvpoun at his pleisoure ; Turnand and Trans-
ferrand, my haill rycht and power thairof, in my said baillie, sua
that he may vse and dispone thairvpoun, and alsua vse and exer-
ceiss this power abouewritten, in all pointis as is aboue expressit,
siclyk, and als frelie in all thingis, as I mycht have done myself
thairintill, gif I were personalie present ; ffirme and stable haldand,
all and quhatsumeuir thingis my said baillie leiffullie dois thairintill,
in tyme cumming, during the said space ; but ony reuocatioune, con-
tradictioune, or agane-calling quhatsumevir : Quhilk power above
writtin, in all thingis as is above expremit, I obleiss me my airis
and successoris, to warrand, acquiet, and defend to the said Robert
Lyndsay, during the space foirsaid, but fraude or gyle. IN WITNESS
heirof, to thir presentis, subscriuit with my hand, my signet is to-
hingin, At Edinburgh the twenti day of Julii, the zeir of God,
Jaj V^c threscore ten zeiris ; before thir witnessis Johne Lyndsay
bruther to the said laird, Robert Ross, Mvngo Schaw, Walter
Colquhon, and Thomas Lizaris.

Attoure I gyff this charge and comission to my fornamit bailye,
on this conditione, at he vait on my lord the erll of Mar,
vithe all my tenentis, and others, at are oblist to my seruice, quhen and quhar he sall be requyrit, be my said Lord
of Mar, be this my hand vryt ; and at he do in all thyngis
to my Lord of Mar, as to my selff, giff I var present.*

JAMES LORD OF TORPHICEN.

* This clause is holograph of Lord Torphichen.

THOMAS LORD BINNING,

His Instrument of Resignation,*

5th October 1615.

𝕴𝖓 𝖙𝖍𝖊 𝕹𝖆𝖒𝖊 𝖔𝖋𝖋 𝕲𝖔𝖉 𝖘𝖔 𝖇𝖊 𝖎𝖙 Be it kend till all men be this present publict instrument, THAT upon the fyft day off October the zeir of GOD one thousand sex hundred and fourtene zeiris, and of the regnes of the richt heich, richt excellent, illuster and michtie prince, JAMES, be the grace of god king off gryt britane, france, and Ireland, defender of the faith, oure souerane lord, the fourtie aucht and tuellf zeiris respective; IN PRESENS off the lordis of his hienes secreit counsall of the kingdome of scotland, haiving his maiesteis full power and comission to ressaue resignatiounes, in his hienes name, being convenit in full nowmer within the laigh counsall hous of the bur^t of edinburg, quhair the saidis lordis ar accustumit to convene in counsall for administratioun of iustice to his hienes liegis, And als in presens of me notar publict, and witnesses vnder written, Compeirit personallie ane nobill and potent lord, Thomas lord Binning secretar to his maiestie of the kingdom of Scotland, And likwayis compeirit personallie James hamiltoun, maisser, procurator to the effect efterspecefit, laufullie constitute, be maister Robert william-soune of muireston, writter, and James lord torphichen, baith with ane consent and assent, be vertue of the letteris obligator maid be thame in favouris of the said Thomas lord binning, anent the alienatioune and dispositioun made be thame, to the said lord bin-ning, his aires and successouris, of all and sindrie the tempill landis tenementis and vthiris efter mentionet, conteining thairintil ane pro-curatorie of resignatioun of the date at edinburgh, the sextene day of september last bypast, registrat in the buikis of Counsall, and decernit to have the strenth of ane act and decreet of the lordis

* From the original in the possession of James Maidment, Esq. Advocate.

thairof, vpoun the sevintene day of the said moneth of september,
And thair the said Thomas lord binning, for himselff personallie,
and the said James hamiltoun as procurator foirsaid, with all hu-
militie and condigne reverence, vpon thair kneyis, as become thame,
Resignit, Surranderit, vpgave and ouirgave, all and sindrie and
quhatsumever temple landis and temple tenementis, pertening to
the said James lord torphichen, ather in propertie or tenandrie
quhairsomevir they ly within this realme of Scotland, ather in
burgh or outwith burgh, in landward or quhilk ar, or may be
knawin to pertene or to haif pertenit to the said lordschip off torphichin at onie tyme bigane, with tenentis, tenandries, service of frie
tennentis, priuiledgis and immunities of the foirsaidis landis and
tenementis quhatsumenir, richteouslie pertening thairto, And quhilkis
the said James lord torphichen and his predecessouris haue enjoyit
and possest or lawfullie micht have enjoyit and possest thir tymes
bypast or contenit in the auld infeftmentis of the lordship of torphichen and sanct Johnne, with castellis, tours, fortalices, houses,
biggingis, orcheardis, zairdis, medowis, parkis, milnis, wodis, fisch-
inges, teindis of the samyn, and all thair pertinentis quhairevir they
ly, Exceptand alwayis sic baroneis, temple landis, kirkis and teindis
as is contenit in the said m^r robert williamsounes infeftment of the
samyn temple landis, quhilk infeftment is of the dait the twentie
thrid day of februar, the zeir of god J.aj.Vj. &c. and nyne zeiris,
Togidder withe the richt and priuiledge of frie regalitie within all
the boundis of the foirsaidis temple landis, with the pertinentis
thairof, respective above specifit, withe all richt, immuniteis and liber-
teis pertening and belanging thereto IN THE HANDIS off the
saidis lordis of his hienes secret counsal his maiesties comissionares
foirsaidis be delyverance of staff and baston as Vse is, in the handis
of ane nobill and michtie erle, alexander, erle of Dunfermline, lord
fyvie and vrquhart, heich chancellair of the said realme of Scotland, for himselff, And in name and behalf of the remanent of
the said lordis of secreit counsall, his maiesties comissionaris above specefit as in the handis of his hienes immediat laufull superior of the
landis and Vthiris above specefit with the pertinentis, IN FAVOURIS
and for new infeftment thairof to be maid and grantit be his
maiestie vnder his hienes gryt seill, to the said nobill lord, Thomas
lord binning, his airis and successouris quhatsumever heritablie,

in dew and competent forme, Togidder with all richt, titill, enteres, and claim of richt, quhilk the saidis m^r Robert williamsoun, James lord torphichen, and Thomas lord binning, or anie of thame, thair airis, or assignayis had, haif, or ony wayes may haif, or claim, thairto, or ony part thairof, in tyme coming: QUHILK resignatioune aboue written being sua maid, as also acceptit and ressavit be the said lord chancellar, for himself, and in name and behalf of the remanent the saidis lordis of secreit counsall, The saidis lordis as his hienes commissionares abovespecifit, gaif, granted, and desponit, to the said nobill lord, Thomas lord binning, his airis and successouris quhatsumever, heritablie, All and sindrie and quhatsomever the foirsaidis temple landis, and temple tenementis, pertening to the said James lord torphichin, ather in propertie or tennandrie quhairsoever they ly within this realme of Scotland, ather in burgh, or outwith burgh, in landwart, and quhilkis ar, or may be knawin to pertene, or to haif pertenit to the said lordship of torphichin, at onie tyme bigane with tennentis, tenandreis, service of frie tennentis, priviledges, and immunities of the foirsaidis landis and tenementis quhatsumever, richteouslie pertaining thairto, And quhilkis the said James lord torphichin and his predicessouris have enjoyit, and possest or laufullie micht have enjoyit and possest, thir tymes bypast, or contenit in the auld infeftmentis of the lordschip of torphichin and sanct Johnne, with castellis, touris, fortalicis, housis, biggingis, orcheardis, zairdis, medowis, parkis, milnis, wodis, fischingis, teindis of the samyn, and all thair pertinentis quhairever they ly (except before exceptit) Togidder with the richt and priviledge of frie regalitie within all the boundis of the foirsaidis temple landis, with the pertinentis thairof, respective above specefit, with all immunities and liberties pertening and belanging thairto: CONFORME to the foirsaidis letteris obligator contening thairintill the said procuratorie of resignatioun, and his hienes infeftment, to be maid and grantit be his maiestie, vnder his hienes gryt seill, to the said nobill lord, Thomas lord binning, and his foirsaidis, thairvpon in all pointis, And yat be deliverance maid be the said lord chancellar of the said staf and baston as vse is in the handis of the said nobill lord Thomas lord binning personalie present and exceptand the samyn: VPOUN the quhilkis all and sindrie the premisses, The said nobill lord, Thomas lord binning, asked and requirit instrumentis and documents, ane or ma, of me notar publict vnder subscryveand, This wes done in the said laich counsall hous of the burgh of Edinburgh betwix nyne and ten houris befoir none, day, moneth, zeir, And of oure said souerane lordis regnis, respective foirsaidis, Befoir thir witnesses James Prymrois, Clerk of secreit counsall, laurence kere, his seruitor, maister Johnne drummond, seruitour to the said lord chancellar, alexander chrystesoune, Notar in edinbur᷑ alexander, and archibald douglasse, maisseris, with diuers vthiris, speciallie callit and requirit at the premises.

Et ego vero magister franciscus hay clericus sancti Andreæ diocesis auctoritate regali notarius publicus ac per dominos consilii secundum tenorem acti parliamenti admissus Quia premissis omnibus et singulis dum sic vt premittitur dicerentur agerentur et fierent vna cum prenominatis testibus presens personaliter interfui Eaque omnia et singula premissa sic fieri et dici vidi scivi audivi ac in notam cepi Ideoque hoc presens publicum instrumentum manu mea fideliter scriptum exinde confeci Signoque nomine et cognomine meis solitis et consuetis signavi et subscripsi in fidem robur et testimonium veritatis omnium et singulorum premissorum Rogatus et requisitus.

MAGISTER FRANCISCUS HAY*
Notarius Publicus.

* In virtue of this resignation, Lord Binning obtained a crown charter of erection of the Temple Lands into a Barony and Regality called Drem ; the charter, precept, (which in those times was generally a separate instrument) and infeftment, were ratified and confirmed bv an act of the Scotish Parliament.

PROCEEDINGS

IN THE

CLAIM for JOHN HAMILTON, Advocate, to the Regality of Drem, comprehending the Temple Lands within the Kingdom of Scotland.

Taken from the Heritable Jurisdiction Papers in the Advocates' Library.

I. PETITION for the Honourable JOHN HAMILTON.

That by charter under the great seal, proceeding upon the resignation of Sir John Anstruther of that Ilk, Baronet, and John Cockburn, then younger of Ormiston (surviving trustees in an Act of Parliament, for vesting in them part of the estate of Thomas Earl of Haddington, and Charles Lord Binning his eldest son, for the purposes therein mentioned,) with consent of Thomas Earl of Haddington, and Charles Lord Binning, both deceased, your petitioner stands heritably vest and seased in all these Temple Lands erected into the free barony and regality of Drem, comprehending *nominatim* several Temple Lands and tenements lying within the town of Edinburgh, the shire of Edinburgh principal, the constabulary of Haddington, the shire of Fife, and a general clause of all other Temple Lands, lying within the realm of Scotland, whether within burgh or without burgh, in landward, excepting always as is excepted forth of Mr *Robert Williamson's* infeftments; and, amongst other clauses is the following: *Tenend. et habend. totas et integras prædictas terras Templarias, tenementa Templaria, aliaque respectivè particulariter et generaliter supra- script. cum pertinen. jacen. modo predict. de nobis nostrisque Regiis successoribus in alba firma, feodo, et hereditate, in perpetuum per omnes rectas metas suas antiquas et diversas prout jacent in longitudine, et latitudine, in domibus, &c. cum curiis, et earum exitibus, herezeldis, bloodwitis, amerciamentis, cum furca et fossa, sock, sack, thoile, thaine, wreck, wair, vert, waith, venisone, in- fang thief, outfang thief, pit and gallows, &c.*

The Temple Lands, which were originally the estate of the Knights of St John of Jerusalem, and have very special privi- leges belonging to them, were at the Reformation erected into a temporal lordship in favours of Lord Torphichen ; and this part of them contained in your petitioner's charter, were disponed by Lord Torphichen, first to Mr Robert Williamson of Muirstoun, and afterwards by the said Lord Torphichen, with consent of Mr Robert Williamson, to Thomas Lord Binning, afterwards Earl of Had- dington, who in the year 1614 resigned them in the hands of the Sovereign for new infeftment, and procured a new charter erecting them into a barony and regality, called *the Barony and Regality of Drem;* and in 1617 had this charter confirmed by Act of Parliament.

That by statute in the 20th year of the reign of his present Majesty, intitled, an act for taking away and abolishing the heri- table jurisdiction in that part of Great Britain called Scotland, and for making satisfaction to the proprietors thereof, &c. it is amongst other things enacted and ordained, " That all heritable jurisdictions " of justiciary, and all regalities and heritable bailieries, &c. " within that part of Great Britain called Scotland, belonging " unto, or possessed or claimed by any subject or subjects, and all " jurisdictions, powers, authorities, and privileges thereunto appurte- " nant or annexed or dependent thereupon, shall be, and they are " hereby from and after the 25th day of March 1748, abrogated, " taken away and totally dissolved and extinguished."

And it is thereby further enacted, " That all jurisdictions, powers " and authorities, legally vested in, or belonging to any such jus- " ticiaries, regalities bailieries, &c. shall from and after the said " 25th day of March, be vested in, and exercised by the Court of " Session, Court of Justiciary at Edinburgh, Judges in the several

" circuits, and the courts of the Sheriffs and Stewarts of shires or
" counties and other the King's courts in Scotland respectively, to
" which such jurisdictions, powers and authorities would now by
" law have belonged, in case such justiciary, regality, bailiary, &c.
" had never been granted or erected."

And it is thereby likewise enacted, " That reasonable and just
" compensation and satisfaction shall be made out of the next aids
" to be granted in Parliament, for and in respect of every such
" justiciary, regality, bailiary, &c. hereby taken away and dissolved,
" or resumed and annexed to the crown, to all and every person or
" persons respectively who shall appear to be lawfully possessed of
" any such justiciary regality or bailiery."

And for obtaining such satisfaction, it is appointed and ordained,
" That all and every person or persons lawfully possessed of any
" such justiciary, regality, bailiary, &c. shall, on or before the 11th
" day of November 1747, make and enter his, her, and their claim
" or claims thereto respectively in the Court of Session in Scot-
" land ; and all such claims, with the titles and vouchers produced
" in support thereof, shall be given out in the usual manner to his
" Majesty's Advocate for Scotland, or his Deputy, or to his Ma-
" jesty's Solicitor General there ; who are hereby authorised to ap-
" pear in behalf of his Majesty, to defend or object against all or
" any such claim or claims, as they shall find cause to oppose, either
" in respect to the validity of the claimant's title to the jurisdiction
" therein set forth, or of the value or price thereof ; and the said
" Court of Session shall in a summary way examine the several
" and respective titles to the same ; and in case they shall find
" any such person or persons to have been so lawfully possessed, as
" aforesaid, of any such justiciary, regality, bailiary, &c. then the
" said Court shall, with all possible dispatch, consider and declare
" their opinion touching the value and price thereof ; and shall
" cause all such opinions to be entered in a roll or book to be kept
" for that purpose, and make certificate or certificates thereof to his
" Majesty, his heirs or successors, in his other Privy Council ; co-
" pies of which shall be laid forthwith before both Houses of Par-
" liament."

That as by the statute above narrated, your petitioner is com-
pelled to accept of such satisfaction for the above mentioned right
and jurisdiction of regality as your Lordships shall value and esti-

mate the same; and as, in order to obtain that satisfaction, the directions of the law must be observed, and the claim entered in due time; your petitioner has taken the liberty to offer this petition to your Lordships, in order that his right and title to the jurisdiction may be cognosced by your Lordships, and the value and worth thereof ascertained.

Your petitioner, whose title to this jurisdiction is vouched by the foresaid charter under the Great Seal proceeding on the resignation of the Earl of Haddington and his trustees, is at some loss to know what to demand as the value and worth thereof; as he believes very few if any instances have occurred where these have been purchased separately by themselves, so they can have no determined value; but as this jurisdiction is very extensive, reaching almost to every corner of Scotland, your petitioner hopes he shall not be thought extravagant in his demands if he shall value it at £3000 sterling.

May it therefore please your Lordships, to find that your petitioner was at the date of the above mentioned Act of Parliament, lawfully possessed of, and entitled to this right of regality; and that he is entitled to the sum of £3000 sterling as the value thereof; and to cause such opinion to be entered in a roll or book to be kept for that purpose, and to make certificate thereof to his Majesty, and his Privy Council, agreeable to the directions of the foresaid statute.

According to Justice, &c.

(Signed)   JOHN HAMILTON.

II. DEFENCES for his MAJESTY's ADVOCATE, against the Claim of Mr JOHN HAMILTON

The claimant, as lord of the regality of Drem, demands £3000.

The regality here claimed is of a pretty singular kind : by the charter, which is in 1614, no particular lands are granted, but in general all the Temple Lands of Scotland, with the exception of these belonging to Mr Robert Williamson, and these belonging to the Preceptor of Torphichen, are granted to Thomas Lord Binning ; and all are erected into one barony and regality, called the Regality of Drem : and in the same form are all the subsequent titles ; so that it does not appear from the claimant's writs, what his territory is, or whether he has any territory at all ; for if there were no Temple Lands in Scotland other than the Lordship of Torphichen, and these which belonged of old to Mr Williamson, then the claimant has no territory at all ; and it is much doubted how far a grant, so extremely vague and uncertain, can be valued ; one thing seems plain, that it could not be sustained as granting any jurisdiction, unless it were shewn, that the particular lands over which it was contended to reach, were truly Temple Lands, or lands which belonged first to the Templars, and then to the Knights of St. John ; and that, it is believed, will be no easy matter at this day.

The respondent, in the second place, must observe, that the charter 1614, ratified in Parliament in the 1617, does not seem sufficient to establish a valid right of regality ; for the Act of Parliament 1633 annuls all regalities of erections, and without entering into the question, whether Temple Lands were Church lands or not, which is a pretty nice dispute, and might be necessary to be canvassed were there a question touching the superiority of Temple Lands, or how far they could be allocate for glebes to ministers or the like, the respondent conceives that the Act 1633 is without exception, and strikes against all regalities over lands which had belonged to suppressed orders, whether these orders were religious, military, or, as was the case of the Templars or Knights of St. John, or Malta, a compound of both ; and if this be so, then the claimant cannot be entituled, unless he support his right by the positive prescription ; and any documents of exercise produced by the claimant hitherto are but imperfect; but as the claimant has obtained a diligence to instruct further, and will then give in a condescendence of the proof of possession, till then it is needless to make any observations upon that point.

The respondent, in the last place, must observe, that the claimant has produced no condescendence what lands belonged to him, either in property or superiority; so that the respondent can form no judgment of the extent of his regality, for which he claims so large a sum as £3000, which, when the claimant does condescend, it is believed will appear excessive.

(Signed)   ALEX. BOSWELL.

February 8th, 1748.

III. CONDESCENDENCE for the Honourable Mr JOHN HAMILTON, Advocate, of the Writs produced by him in support of his Claim for the Regality of Drem, and for instructing the Exercise and Possession of the said Jurisdiction.

1609.
Feb. 23.

Charter under the Great Seal in favours of Mr Robert Williamson of Murehouse. " Dedisse, &c. omnes et singulas et omnes et " quascunque terras Templarias et tenementa dicto Jacobo domino " de Torphichen aut in proprietate seu tenendria spectan. et per- " tinen. ubicunque infra regnum nostrum Scotiæ jacen. tam infra " burgos, quam extra rure, quæ ad Dominium de Torphichen seu " ad Preceptoream ejusdem, dignoscuntur pertinere, &c. &c. quæ dic- " tus Jacobus Dominus de Torphichen seu de Sanct. Johanne, " ullo tempore prædicto possiderunt, aut in possessione fuerunt, aut " in antiquis infeofamentis seu ejusdem erectionibus content."— From which the following lands are excepted:—The lands and baronies of Torphichen, Liston, Denny, Thankerton, Ballintrude, Maryculter and Kincardine, Stanhope, Peaston, Temple-priest and Temple-lands in Corstorphin, Halkerston, Bylawknow, Castleton, Snyps and Dennyside, Halkerston, Knyghton lie Temple Lands de Lamington, the Temple Lands of Langton, Harperrig and Kirknewton, as reserved by and belonging to the Lord Torphichen, and containing a clause of Novodamus.

Charters proceeding upon the resignation of Lord Torphichen and Mr Robert Williamson, in favour of Thomas Lord Binning, his Majesty's Secretary of State for Scotland, of the foresaid whole Temple Lands as mentioned in Mr Robert Williamson's charter; and the Temple Lands within the shire of Edinburgh principal, Haddington and Fife, are particularly mentioned and enumerate, containing a clause of novodamus and erection of the foresaid whole Temple Lands " in unam integram et liberam baroniam et regali- " tatem de Drem nunc et omni tempore futuro nuncupand." *(1614. Feb. 23. Oct. 13.)*

Ratification in Parliament, whereby " his Majesty's Estates of " Parliament ratify and approve the infeftment made and granted " by his Majesty to his Hieness's traist cousigne and counsellor " Thomas Lord Binning, Secretar to his Majesty, and President " of his Hieness's College of Justice of the samen kingdom, his " aires, &c. heritably, of all and sundrie the Tempill Landis et Tem- " pill-tenementis pertaining of befoir to James Lord Torphichen in " propertie or tenandrie quhaire-evir the samen lye within the said " Kingdom of Scotland, als weill within burgh as without burgh " in landwart, &c. in all and sundry heidis, arteclis, clausis," &c. with the precept and instrument of sasine following thereupon. *(June 8. 1617.)*

Charter under the Great Seal in favours of the said Mr John Hamilton, claimant, proceeding upon the resignation of the trustees appointed by Act of Parliament for selling part of the estate of Thomas Earl of Haddington. *(Feb. 12. 1736.)*

Instrument of Seisin thereon. *(Jan. 23. 1746.)*

For instructing the Exercise and Possession of the said Regality, there is produced :—

Temple Court Books for the shire of Edinburgh principal, Leith, Constabulary of Haddington, shires of Stirling, Peebles, Lanark, Anandale, Dumfries and stewartry of Kirkcudbright, shires of Kincardine, Linlithgow, Aberdeen, Bamff; wherein the several Temple vassals within each county, stewartry, and constabulary above mentioned, are all particularly mentioned and engrossed, beginning 23d Augt. 1614. Ending anno 1615.

List of the Temple vassals relative to the foresaid court book, who had not produced their charters.

Nov. 3. 1618.
Nov. 15. 1618.
Court of the Temple Lands within the shire of Bamff.
Court of the Temple Lands within the shire of Dumbarton.
Temple Court Book beginning 8th June 1710, and ending 24th August 1731, wherein the vassals from several counties compear, and give suit and presence in the said court, produce their writs, and the Bailie ordaining the cross of St. John to be affixed on the Temple Lands within burgh, and amerciating such as did not affix the said cross.

2d February 1748.

A PETITION was presented by the Hon. Mr John Hamilton for a diligence against witnesses and havers, " for recovering the title " deeds necessary to support his claim, and for bringing farther proof " of the exercise and possession of the jurisdiction claimed."

The Prayer of this petition appears to have been granted ; but no mention is made in the notes of proof having been led, or of the result.

IV. Unto the Right Honourable the Lords of Council and Session, the MEMORIAL of Mr JOHN HAMILTON, Advocate ;

March 1748.

Humbly sheweth,

That the memorialist is by your Lorships found entitled to the jurisdiction of the regality of Drem, which comprehends the whole lands in Scotland (excepting the Lordship of Torphichen, and some other lands and baronies specified in his rights) which belonged to the ancient order of Knights Templars, and afterwards to the order of St. John of Jerusalem ; a territory extremely extensive, there being few shires or burghs in Scotland where there are not parts of them subject to this jurisdiction.

The extent of this regality, and its being over tenements in so many different shires and burghs, are doubtless considerations which must make it appear more valuable, as it gives it a more diffusive interest, and that the proprietor of other jurisdictions within which part of the memorialist's regality did locally lie, would doubtless have purchased his jurisdiction from him over these parts, at a rate far above what people would pay for a jurisdiction of regality, over a separate and detached territory, as it is like a few aikers within the inclosures of others.

These considerations, which make this regality appear singularly valuable, and distinguish it from all other regalities claimed, it is humbly hoped will be specially under the eye of the Court in estimating the satisfaction to be given to the memorialist; and it is the more necessary that it should be so, that truly if the rule for estimating other regalities were to be followed in this case, he should be in a manner cut out from any satisfaction for being deprived of his valuable jurisdiction to which your Lorships have found him entitled. For the case happens, that the valuations of the tenements subject to this regality are for most part *in cumulo* with other lands not subject thereto, and no distinction made in the cess books betwixt *Temple* and other lands, and to get them disjoined would be a work of great labour, and of more time than can now be spared. But certain it is that the valuation would come to be high: For within the city of Edinburgh alone the tenements subject to this regality are £6302 Scots of valued rent, as appears from a certificate produced; and these tenements are but a small pendicle of the territory.

In this state it is hoped your Lordships will not think it reasonable or just that the memorialist (who were he prepared to give in a full valuation, as is humbly conceived, for the reasons mentioned above might be entitled to a satisfaction upon a higher medium than other lords of regality) should be totally cut out, because he is not in condition to point out this valuation of his territory.

This will doubtless occur to your Lordships, that jurisdictions are to be exercised over persons, and there are more inhabitants upon some aikers of the memorialist's territories than will be found upon many miles of other regalities, and the jurisdiction that he has over parts of many burghs, does in some manner make him in the case of other officers whom the Court has found entitled to a price, not upon the plan of valuation, but upon a reasonable estimate of the honour and interest attending these offices; and, with great submission, there seems to be the same reason for such rule being followed in this case, a Lord of Regality being honourable, and his power and interest over his territory being very considerable, particularly in this case, where the privileges are as great and extensive, if not more so, than any other regality in Scotland.

The Court sustained Mr Hamilton's right to the Heritable Office of the Lordship and Jurisdiction of the Regality of Drem, and allowed him £500 as a suitable remuneration.*

Lord Elchies, from whose Collection of the Jurisdiction Papers, the claim has been procured, has preserved a state of the vote upon the question of sustaining Mr Hamilton's title : it was as follows :—

For the claim, Lords Elchies, Drummore, Haining, Arniston, Monzie, Shewalton.

Contra, Dun, &c.

Non liquet, Lords Strichen, Murkle.

* Acts of Sederunt, p. 428.